D0477450

A CELEBRATION OF
100 YEARS
OF SQUASH
AT PALL MALL

JOHN HOPKINS

ROYAL AUTOMOBILE CLUB
IN ASSOCIATION WITH LENNARD PUBLISHING

A CELEBRATION OF 100 YEARS OF SQUASH AT PALL MALL

This book has been produced for the Royal Automobile Club
by Lennard Books
a division of Lennard Associates Ltd
Windmill Cottage, Mackerye End
Harpenden, Herts AL5 5DR

Text © John Hopkins 2011

This edition first published in the UK in 2011
by the Royal Automobile Club in association with Lennard Publishing

ISBN 978 1 85291 152 2

Production Editor: Chris Marshall
Designer: Paul Cooper
Jacket Design: Paul Cooper
Printed and bound in Britain by Butler Tanner & Dennis Ltd

AUTHOR'S ACKNOWLEDGEMENT
Though I am the author of this book, two men helped me enormously, giving up days to reading my copy and helping to shape it as well as undertaking the search for photographs and compiling the appendix. The Club owes Chris Orriss and Maurice Glover a huge debt of gratitude for making this book as good as it is and so do I.

This book is dedicated to my father, who is older than the Pall Mall clubhouse.

PICTURE ACKNOWLEDGEMENTS
All the illustrations in this book have been supplied by the Royal Automobile Club and the Club is very grateful to Maurice Glover and Paul Cooper for the photographs that they took especially for this book. The Club would also like to acknowledge the contributions of Hamilton Ford (p5), Stephen Line (p11) and Robin Eley Jones (p71). Best endeavours have been made to source and secure copyright clearance for all other photographs used but in the event of any copyright owner being overlooked please address correspondence to Lennard Associates Ltd, Windmill Cottage, Mackerye End, Harpenden, Herts AL5 5DR

Contents

Message from the President   4

Foreword   5

Spirit of Pall Mall   6

The First Fifty Years   22

Since the Sixties   40

The Professionals   62

Ten of the Best   80

The Trophy Cabinet   102

Afterword   120

Appendix   122

I am delighted to write a foreword to this history of squash at the Pall Mall clubhouse of the Royal Automobile Club. As President of the Club, with fond memories of being taught squash there myself by the then Club Professional, Jack Giles, I am only too aware of the considerable role of the Club in the development of the game.

It was at the Pall Mall clubhouse that the Squash Rackets Association first met in December 1928, among them a sizeable number of Club members. The relationship between the Club and the Association has remained a close one. The Royal Automobile Club inaugurated the Drysdale Cup and has a thriving constituency of Squash-playing members.

I congratulate the Club on the Centenary of the Pall Mall clubhouse and upon its contribution to the development of Squash.

Foreword

One of the things that defines and distinguishes the Royal Automobile Club is that it has always been a sporting club. Not a sports club in today's sense, but a club formed for the pursuit of motor sport and with exercise and games in several forms at its core. Squash has been central to Club life from the beginning and we now celebrate 100 years of the game within the wondrous Pall Mall clubhouse with the publication of a book about it.

It's not just the playing of squash that makes the game special at this club, creating such a vibrant community today and making this book worth writing. It's the context in which it's played: the people, the surroundings, the drinks, the laughs, the stories, the continuity, the spirit. To capture this spirit was always going to be difficult. We felt it should come from within the membership and it seemed fortunate and fitting that we could call on John Hopkins, who joined the Club in 1963 and has been a sportswriter on *The Sunday Times* and *The Times* for the past 40 years, to piece it together.

John started watching and playing squash at the Club in 1965 and was soon writing about it in newspapers and magazines. He joined the squash committee in 1969, was chairman from 1978 to 1995 and for much of this time was also editor of *Pell-Mell & Woodcote*, the Club magazine. He ran our Bath Club Cup team for a short while and when the Club entered a second team, played in that from time to time.

It was clear to the current committee that John had the voice with which to tell the story of Club squash, having himself been a part of it for very near half of our 100 years.

Over to you John.

James Sandwith
Chairman – Pall Mall Squash Committee

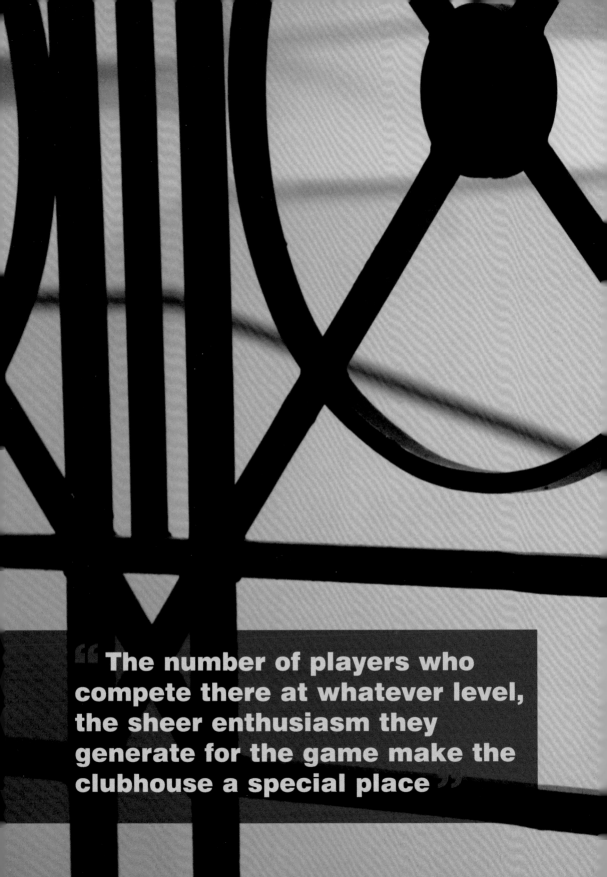

" **The number of players who compete there at whatever level, the sheer enthusiasm they generate for the game make the clubhouse a special place**

Spirit of
Pall Mall

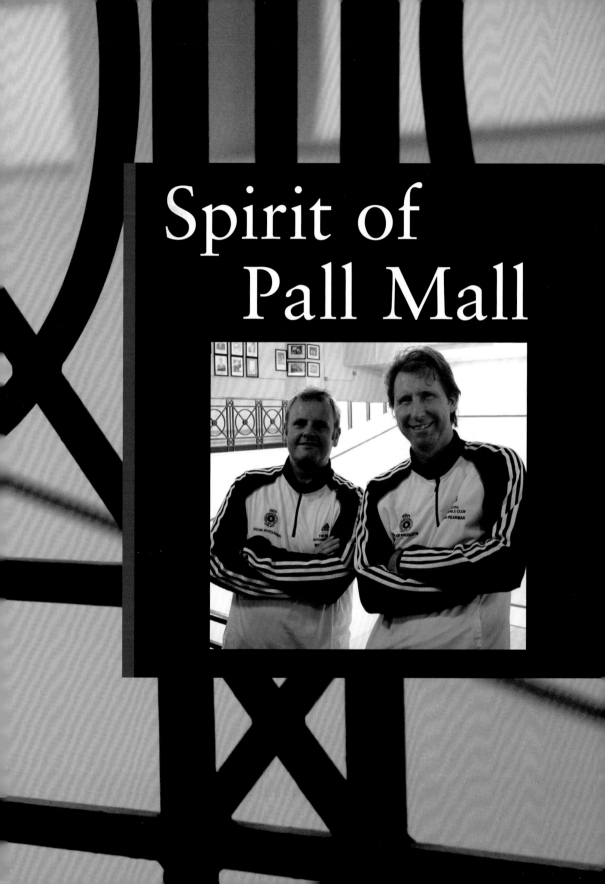

One night in October 2010 a group of squash-playing members sat down to dinner in the Long Bar of the Pall Mall clubhouse. If this conjures up an image in the mind's eye of fit young men, all in their twenties, forget it. This was a Royal Automobile Club veterans team (over 45s in other words) that had played a match in the Bath Club Cup against the veterans of the Cumberland Club. Some still had the half-century to face while others were in their fifties and some their sixties. Were they having a good time? To a man they said yes.

This made me realise not only that squash at the Club was thriving but also why it was. As the clubhouse at Pall Mall begins its second century, the game is proving more appealing to more members than at any time in the Club's history because a particularly difficult trick has been pulled off: the existing and considerable history of squash at the Royal Automobile Club is now complemented by an enhanced squash-playing experience, courtesy of the management and successive squash committees. No

Early days. Squash derives from rackets, which began in London's debtors' gaols in the 1700s and is mentioned in Dickens's Pickwick Papers, in which Mr Pickwick is consigned to the Fleet Prison.

matter how old they are, the Club's players have come to realise that a good thrash around on court in congenial surroundings, where enjoyment of the food and the company is as important as the squash itself, is worth doing, even at an advanced age and even when there is a risk of physical damage.

Squash has been played for a long time. It started as rackets in the debtors' prisons in London and spread to Harrow School in Victorian England, arriving at Pall Mall when the clubhouse opened in 1911. Between that date and this we have had plenty of time to appreciate its appeal as a means of physically exhausting oneself in a short space of time, one of many virtues that caused the game to spread like wildfire in the 1960s and 1970s. 'Squash at its best is a combination of supreme physical fitness, intelligence and self-control,' Brian Jeffries, the writer, put it in an article in *The Sunday Times* in 1971. 'But even for the average player, to conquer an opponent that little bit better than yourself can add a new dimension to life. To walk back to the changing room as weak as a kitten, with the sweat dripping off you but with your mind as clear as tomorrow's dawn, is better than five reefers or a trip on LSD. There is no hang up. It is the ideal therapy for tired businessmen and frustrated workers.'

The emergence of Jonah Barrington as squash's dominant figure in Britain helped the game expand quickly. 'By 1970 when he had won the British Open (the de facto world championship) three times, he was the best in the world,' I wrote in *Sports World* magazine in 1974. His biblical Christian name helped. So did his lifestyle during his early days. Celibate, teetotal and talkative as ever he was, he declared himself regularly to be 'the only monk in South Kensington'. The better Jonah became, the more publicity he attracted, which boosted squash more. 'By this time the game's growth resembled a cheese rolling downhill, gathering impetus all the time,' I continued. 'Three hundred thousand players, five hundred thousand, seven hundred thousand? Nobody actually counted them yet nobody had any figures to dispute the claims.' A report published in April 1974 by the Squash Rackets Association (SRA) claimed that squash would rival soccer as a major sport in Britain in seven years, a claim that seemed a trifle far-fetched even then.

The Club has huge significance ... Pall Mall is to squash what Lord's is to cricket

At Pall Mall, the playing of squash is only the half of it. The Club has huge significance in the historical development of the game, as will become clear in future chapters. Pall Mall is to squash what Lord's is to cricket. The clubhouse was the site in the early 1920s of the first meetings of the body set up to administer competitive squash, a sub-committee of the Tennis & Rackets Association. The Club provided a team for the Bath Club Cup, London's premier inter-club competition, when it began in 1922. The Club's assistant secretary took the minutes of the SRA after it was formed in 1928, and SRA committee meetings were held at Pall Mall for years. When the SRA ran into financial difficulties it was the Club's auditors who provided the expertise to help the association out of its troubles, while in 2002 the Club came to the rescue of the British Open Championship when at the last minute the competition lost most of its sponsors. The Club made a donation of £10,000 towards a shortfall of £50,000 and this was sufficient to encourage other last-minute saviours to step in and ensure the event went ahead.

As a venue for competitive squash, the Pall Mall clubhouse takes some beating. Down the years, the Open and the Amateur Championship have been held at the Club, the Open when it was to all intents and purposes the world championship. The Club has also hosted the Strawson Memorial match between the Jesters Club and the game's governing body, the annual match between the men and women of Oxford and Cambridge Universities, the Drysdale Cup for boys under 19, the Londonderry Cup, the school Old Boys team event and now the Jesters Trophy, the continuation of the Amateur Championship. The Club has a sense of squash history that is almost palpable, and there is still considerable reverence for the past within the squash section at Pall Mall. Old trophies, books and other memorabilia can be seen around the squash area. Handsome honours boards hang on walls in the changing room and corridors. The past may be a foreign country, as L.P. Hartley wrote in *The Go-Between*, but it is very visible in this quarter of the Royal Automobile Club.

Stuart Courtney first passed through the revolving door at Pall Mall in 1965. He was just 16 and was on his way to play in the Drysdale Cup for the first time. 'I was bowled over,' Courtney said. 'In no way was

SQUASH RACQUETS COMMITTEE.

A meeting of this Committee was held on Friday, 29th September, 1922, at 6 o'clock, when there were present: Col. R.E.B. Crompton,C.B. (Chairman), Mr. Sanwyer Atkin, Mr. C.F. Cross, Dr. T. Drysdale, Mr. E.W. Fordham, Mr. S. Vernon Harcourt, Mr. P. Wilkins, the Deputy Secretary and the Clerk to Committees.

MINUTES.--The minutes of the last meeting were read, confirmed, and signed by the Chairman.

INTER-CLUB MEETING AT BATH CLUB.--The Chairman reported that he and Mr. Harcourt had attended the meeting at the Bath Club on the 28th September. Six Clubs were represented and the following points were settled:--

(a) Three players for 1922 instead of 5.

(b) A competitor to name his Club for the year and to be ineligible to play for any other Club that year.

(c) The times when matches would be held.

(d) Each match won to count 1 point (best of 3 games), i.e., 3 points can be obtained on ine Inter-Club match.

(e) If two Clubs are equal at the end of the season the deciding match to be played in a neutral court. Any difficulty as to the neutral court to be settled by the Secretary of the Association.

(f) A Committee to be appointed for the standardisation of recquets.

The Chairman said that he thought the F.A.C. standardised ball would be adopted by the other Clubs, including Queen's. As regards Lord's the question remained unsettled.

ELECTION OF CAPTAIN.--On the motion of Mr. Fordham, seconded by Mr. Cross, it was unanimously resolved:--

That Dr. T. Drysdale be elected Captain for the ensuing year and that the selection of teams be left to him.

REGULATIONS.--The Committee agreed to the following alterations:--

(See copy inserted in the Minute Book.)

ADMISSION OF LADIES TO SQUASH RACQUET GALLERY.--A letter from Mr. Frank M. Strawson suggesting that ladies be admitted on Saturdays instead of Fridays was read and referred to the House Committee with the recommendation that the suggestion be adopted.

WINTER TOURNAMENT HANDICAPS.--Mr. Harcourt raised this question. After some discussion it was agreed that further consideration be given to it at the next meeting.

MEETINGS OF COMMITTEE.--Agreed that a monthly meeting of the Committee be held on the last Friday in each month, at 6 o'clock.

..............................Chairman.

Date.....27 Oct.........1922.

FACING PAGE: *The Royal Automobile Club squash committee minutes for 29 September 1922 report agreement on some conditions of play for the new inter-club competition that became the Bath Club Cup.* RIGHT: *Erstwhile rivals Chris Orriss and Stuart Courtney still grappling over the Drysdale Cup, 40 years on from their meeting in the 1965/66 final.* BELOW RIGHT: *The Drysdale Cup board bearing the names of the squash greats cited by Courtney. He added his name to the roll of honour in 1967.*

I prepared for what I saw or the history of the place. As a youngster I was completely in awe of it. When I played the final against Chris Orriss the next year my mother had to be smuggled in through a back door to come and watch me play. Because I later won the Drysdale I was excused having to pay the joining fee to become a member. I paid only the subscription. Actually, my father paid that until I was working and could afford it for myself. It meant that now I was a member of this fantastic club.

'But it took ages for me to get to grips with it. I looked at the boards. I am a bit of a sports history buff and I really got into the history. I saw my name on the Drysdale Cup winners' board alongside names like [Nigel] Broomfield, [Mike] Oddy, [Jeremy] Lyon and [Mike] Corby – some of the greatest names in the game. When I talked to other Bath Club Cup players I found they all wanted to come to the Club. There was this sense of

DRYSDALE CUP COMPETITION	
1926 C.J.WILSON, (REPTON).	1948 D.W.SWALES, (LANCING).
1927 C.J.WILSON, (REPTON).	1949 M.G.CASE, (MARLBOROUGH).
1928 K.A.WAGG, (ETON).	1950 M.G.CASE, (MARLBOROUGH).
1929 J.N.S.RIDGERS, (WELLINGTON).	1951 W.J.DOWNEY, (SEDBERGH).
1930 E.NOEL EVANS, (HAILEYBURY).	1952 N.H.R.A.BROOMFIELD, (HAILEYBURY).
1931 J.A.GILLIES, (WINCHESTER).	1953 J.G.A.LYON, (LANCING).
1932 R.W.BEADLE, (MARLBOROUGH).	1954 N.H.R.A.BROOMFIELD, (HAILEYBURY).
1933 N.W.D.YARDLEY, (ST PETER'S YORK).	1955 N.H.R.A.BROOMFIELD, (HAILEYBURY).
1934 N.W.D.YARDLEY, (ST PETER'S YORK).	1956 M.A.ODDY, (LATE RUGBY).
1935 G.S.PANCHAUD, (LANCING).	1957 D.JUDE, (LATE LANCING).
1936 C.M.BUTLER, (LANCING).	1958 D.I.MEDWAY, (LATE CHELTENHAM)
1937 R.S.WOODWARD, (LANCING).	1959 M.W.CORBY, (LATE MILL HILL)
1938 D.G.YEATS BROWN, (TONBRIDGE).	1960 D.R.BRAZIER, (LANCING).
1939 A.AITCHISON, (MED.SCH.MIDDLESEX HOSP).	1961 P.GERLOW, (COPENHAGEN).
1940 to 1946, (NO COMPETITION).	1962 P.GERLOW, (COPENHAGEN).
1947 J.R.BARRINGTON, (BRIGHTON).	1963 M.S.KHAN, (MILLFIELD).

history. Amr Bey played here. Oke Johnson taught here. Nigel Broomfield played here. It is hard for me to describe what it was like to be admitted to this great place. Sometimes then I had to pinch myself to make sure I wasn't dreaming. In due course, I played in some of the same matches as Broomfield and afterwards we had dinner together and just as he told stories of being in the Foreign Office, James Hunt regaled us with stories of Formula 1. I really thought to myself, "Wow! This place is something else."'

Happily, many others have found as much to their liking at Pall Mall as Stuart Courtney, even if they might not be able to express it so clearly. The number of players who compete there at whatever level, the sheer enthusiasm they generate for the game make the clubhouse a special place. At the Royal Automobile Club, if not in many other places, squash is thriving. There are more than 1200 players, more than 40 leagues with five players in each plus a waiting list to join the leagues, and two full-time teaching pros as well as a part-time lady professional. The clubhouse has three singles courts and one doubles court, and the Club boasts a fixture list that is the envy of any club.

How can this be? Why is Pall Mall so successful? Was it because in January 2005 the Club decided to cease charging for sports facilities, which included squash? Although members continued to pay the pros for a lesson, they no longer had to pay a court fee. Like the abolition of entrance fees to museums, this was a decision that was a long time in coming, but rather surprisingly it had only a marginal effect on numbers playing squash at Pall Mall.

No, the answers lie elsewhere. First, it is important to realise that the appeal of squash has never changed, though its popularity might have diminished. It has always

THE ROYAL AUTOMOBILE CLUB
SQUASH RACKETS COMMITTEE
PALL MALL

2010–2011

James Sandwith (Chairman)
Dominic Curtis
Maurice Glover
Simon Lambert
Michael Metcalfe
Chris Orriss
Nick Clapp
Graham Nichols

SQUASH RACKETS FIXTURES
2010–2011

HEAD PROFESSIONAL
Greg Pearman

ASSISTANTS
Mark Jackson
Lauren Briggs

Maurice Glover
Fixtures Secretary

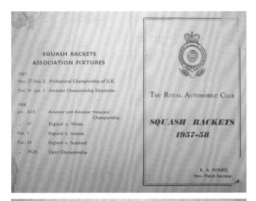

Day	Date		Opponents	Courts	Time(pm)	Team Manager	Results For	Against
Tue	14 Sep		Londonderry Cup Final	RAC	7:00	James Sandwith		
Wed	6 Oct	D	RAC VETS v Roehampton	RAC	7:00	Chris Orriss		
Wed	6 Oct		Roehampton 3 v RAC 2	Away	7:00	Jeremy Krzystyniak		
Thu	7 Oct		RAC 1 v Roehampton 1	RAC	7:00	James Sandwith		
Fri	8 Oct		Australian Defence Force touring team	RAC	7:00	James Sandwith		
Wed	13 Oct		Hurlingham v RAC VETS	Away	7:00	Chris Orriss		
Wed	13 Oct		RAC 2 v Hurlingham 3	RAC	7:00	Jeremy Krzystyniak		
Thu	14 Oct		Hurlingham 1 v RAC 1	Away	7:00	James Sandwith		
Tue	19 Oct		RAC v The Army	RAC	7:00	Roland Steere		
Wed	20 Oct		Queen's 2 v RAC 2	Away	7:00	Jeremy Krzystyniak		
Wed	20 Oct	D	RAC VETS v Cumberland	RAC	7:00	Chris Orriss		
Thu	21 Oct		RAC 1 v Oxford & Cambridge 'A'	RAC	7:00	James Sandwith		
Mon	25 Oct		Hurlingham Under 35's v RAC Under 35's	Away	7:00	Nick Clapp		
Wed	27 Oct		RAC 2 v Cumberland 2	RAC	7:00	Jeremy Krzystyniak		
Thu	28 Oct		Cumberland 1 v RAC 1	Away	7:00	James Sandwith		
Tue	2 Nov		RAC v Royal Navy	RAC	7:00	Gorm Nielsen		
Wed	3 Nov		Oxford & Cambridge v RAC VETS	Away	7:00	Chris Orriss		
Wed	3 Nov		RAC 2 v Oxford & Cambridge 3	RAC	7:00	Jeremy Krzystyniak		
Mon	8 Nov		RAC Under 35's v Old Etonians Under 35's	RAC	7:00	Nick Clapp		
Tue	9 Nov		RAC v RAF	RAC	7:00	Andrew Stimpson		
Wed	10 Nov		R.A.F. v RAC 2	Away	7:00	Jeremy Krzystyniak		
Wed	10 Nov	D	RAC VETS v Wimbledon Lakeside	RAC	7:00	Chris Orriss		
Thu	11 Nov		RAC 1 v H.A.C.	RAC	7:00	James Sandwith		
Mon	15 Nov		RAC v Old Bradfieldians	RAC	7:00	Darab Khan		
Wed	17 Nov		RAC 2 v Queen's 3	RAC	7:00	Jeremy Krzystyniak		
Thu	18 Nov		Oxford & Cambridge 'B' v RAC 1	Away	7:00	James Sandwith		
Mon	22 Nov		Ealing SRC v RAC	Away	7:00	Chris Lowry		
Tue	23 Nov	D	RAC v The Swans	RAC	7:00	Alan Catling		
Wed	24 Nov		Hurlingham 2 v RAC 2	Away	7:00	Jeremy Krzystyniak		
Thu	25 Nov		RAC 1 v Bath & Racquets	RAC	7:00	James Sandwith		
Tue	30 Nov		RAC v The Escorts	RAC	7:00	Bill Higson		
Wed	1 Dec		Queen's v RAC VETS	Away	7:00	Chris Orriss		
Wed	1 Dec		RAC 2 v Roehampton 2	RAC	7:00	Jeremy Krzystyniak		
Thu	2 Dec		Queen's 1 v RAC 1	Away	7:00	James Sandwith		
Wed	8 Dec		Lansdowne 2 v RAC 2	Away	7:00	Jeremy Krzystyniak		
Wed	8 Dec		M.C.C. v RAC VETS	Away	7:00	Chris Orriss		
Thu	9 Dec		RAC 1 v Lansdowne 1	RAC	7:00	James Sandwith		
Tue	14 Dec		John Lewis v RAC	Away	7:00	Nick Clapp		
Wed	15 Dec		RAC 2 v M.C.C. 2	RAC	7:00	Jeremy Krzystyniak		
Thu	16 Dec		M.C.C. 1 v RAC 1	Away	7:00	James Sandwith		
2011								
Tue	11 Jan		RAC v Jesters	RAC	7:00	James Sandwith		
Wed	12 Jan		RAC 2 v Roehampton 3	RAC	7:00	Jeremy Krzystyniak		
Wed	12 Jan		Roehampton v RAC VETS	Away	7:00	Chris Orriss		
Thu	13 Jan		Roehampton 1 v RAC 1	Away	7:00	James Sandwith		
Mon	17 Jan	D	Jesters v Escorts	RAC	7:00	Bill Higson		
Wed	19 Jan		Hurlingham 3 v RAC 2	Away	7:00	Jeremy Krzystyniak		
Wed	19 Jan	D	RAC VETS v Hurlingham	RAC	7:00	Chris Orriss		
Thu	20 Jan		RAC 1 v Hurlingham 1	RAC	7:00	James Sandwith		
Mon	24 Jan		RAC v Cambridge University	RAC	7:00	Roland Steere		
Wed	26 Jan		Cumberland v RAC VETS	Away	7:00	Chris Orriss		
Wed	26 Jan		RAC 2 v Queen's 2	RAC	7:00	Jeremy Krzystyniak		
Thu	27 Jan		Oxford & Cambridge 'A' v RAC 1	Away	7:00	James Sandwith		
Sat	29 Jan							
Sun	30 Jan		Jesters British Amateur Open Championship	RAC				
Mon	31 Jan							
Mon	14 Feb		RAC v Oxford University	RAC	7:00	Roland Steere		
Tue	15 Feb		RAC v Lloyds	RAC	7:00	Andrew Lowenthal		
Wed	2 Feb		Cumberland 2 v RAC 2	Away	7:00	Jeremy Krzystyniak		
Thu	3 Feb		RAC 1 v Cumberland 1	RAC	7:00	James Sandwith		
Wed	9 Feb		Oxford & Cambridge 3 v RAC 2	Away	7:00	Jeremy Krzystyniak		
Wed	9 Feb	D	RAC VETS v Oxford & Cambridge	RAC	7:00	Chris Orriss		
Wed	16 Feb		RAC 2 v R.A.F.	RAC	7:00	Jeremy Krzystyniak		
Wed	16 Feb		Wimbledon Lakeside v RAC VETS	Away	7:00	Chris Orriss		
Thu	17 Feb		H.A.C. v RAC 1	Away	7:00	James Sandwith		
Sat	19 Feb		Oxford & Cambridge Varsity Match Ladies commence at 1pm and will be followed by gentlemen at 4pm	RAC				
Tue	22 Feb	D	Alma Doubles	RAC	7:00	Chris Lowry		
Wed	23 Feb		Queen's 3 v RAC 2	Away	7:00	Jeremy Krzystyniak		
Thu	24 Feb		RAC 1 v Oxford & Cambridge 'B'	RAC	7:00	James Sandwith		
Wed	2 Mar		RAC 2 v Hurlingham 2	RAC	7:00	Jeremy Krzystyniak		
Thu	3 Mar		Bath & Racquets v RAC 1	Away	7:00	James Sandwith		
Wed	9 Mar	D	RAC VETS v Queen's	RAC	7:00	Chris Orriss		
Wed	9 Mar		Roehampton 2 v RAC 2	Away	7:00	Jeremy Krzystyniak		
Thu	10 Mar		RAC 1 v Queen's 1	RAC	7:00	James Sandwith		
Mon	14 Mar	D	Jesters v All England	RAC	6:00	James Sandwith		
Wed	16 Mar		RAC 2 v Lansdowne 2	RAC	7:00	Jeremy Krzystyniak		
Thu	17 Mar		Lansdowne 1 v RAC 1	Away	7:00	James Sandwith		
Tue	22 Mar		RAC v Ealing SRC	RAC	7:00	Chris Lowry		
Wed	23 Mar		M.C.C. 2 v RAC 2	Away	7:00	Jeremy Krzystyniak		
Thu	24 Mar		RAC 1 v M.C.C. 1	RAC	7:00	James Sandwith		
Wed	30 Mar	D	RAC VETS v M.C.C.	RAC	7:00	Chris Orriss		
Mon	28 Mar		Old Etonians Under 35's v RAC under 35's	Away	7:00	Nick Clapp		
Tue	29 Mar	D	RAC v The Veterans SRC of Great Britain	RAC	7:00	Chris Orriss		
Tue	5 Apr		RAC Under 35's v Hurlingham Under 35's	RAC	7:00	Nick Clapp		
Wed	13 Apr	D	Finals Night & Centenary Dinner	RAC	6:00			
Tue	19 Apr	D	RAC v Old Tonbridgians	RAC	7:00	Simon Lambert		
Tue	3 May		RAC v John Lewis	RAC	7:00	Nick Clapp		
Thu	12 May	D	Interclubhouse Doubles	WCP	6:30	Simon Lambert		

Red denotes Bath Club Cup.

THIS PAGE AND FACING PAGE: 'A fixture list that is the envy of any club.' A little more crowded than it was in 1957/58, the 2010/11 fixture card nevertheless still pits the Royal Automobile Club against the cream of squash in the Home Counties and beyond. Red type still denotes a Bath Club Cup match, while D for dinner on the older card has become D for doubles today.

been perceived as a gentlemanly game and this endures still. 'To me it was THE sport where people did not cheat,' Laurie Lowenthal, a businessman who played at the Club before hanging up his racket in 1984, said in 1980. 'If the ball was not up they would say it was not up ... It's just you and your conscience against another player and his conscience and I liked that very much.'

'Frankly there are three things in my life which if I had to give them up would constitute a tragedy,' Lowenthal continued. 'They are, and not necessarily in this order, good food and drink, sex and squash. As far as I am concerned one affects the other. I love going on holiday but if I am away for more than two weeks and I don't play squash then I start to miss it. I play squash to get the sluggishness out of my system ... It's a funny thing and I don't know how to explain it but squash enables me to do all the things that other normal people do without playing the game.

It's just you and your conscience against another player and his conscience and I liked that very much

'Because I took it up late I am still learning. Suddenly I discover I can play a new shot, a shot I couldn't play a year ago. It's a rare game at which you can still be making discoveries when you've been playing it for over 30 years. It is certainly not true of tennis. I find tennis a more difficult game than squash. There is the net and all those lines. At squash you have more time. If you make a mistake and the other chap doesn't kill it, you can recover. You can't at tennis. Once you hit it out, you have hit it out.'

Squash also remains a game that usually takes less than an hour and can be played at courts that are often near the office. So one tries to make time for it. What has changed, however, is that certain key people at the Club have helped to establish conditions in which the maximum amount of enjoyment can be had in the minimum time. The result has been that players of all ages continue to pound away on court – and make their way upstairs for a restoring drink or meal afterwards. 'I play squash so that I can eat this,' Professor Andrew Nicholson, 48, said that October night in the Long Bar as he stared down happily at a plate of *Apfelstrudel* and ice cream. 'I don't eat puddings at home but I feel that if I have just played

squash then I can get away with this. Besides, I like the ambience. Yes, I feel stiff the morning after a game, and yes, I have to stretch before and after a game. But it is worth it. My age is an opponent not to be given into.'

RIGHT: *Andrew Nicholson, an enthusiast determined not to be defeated by age.* BELOW RIGHT: *Jim Markwick, another supporter of squash at Pall Mall and of the unique ambience and atmosphere with which it is imbued.*

Getting this balance right between providing squash and providing squash in a congenial atmosphere is what has proved so tricky. The squash clubs that sprang up in the Barrington boom days and immediately thereafter thought that to provide courts was enough. It might have been then, but once people realised how much physical stress squash can put on a person, and doctors started expressing concerns about the dangers of the sport, then the flight from squash began. Many clubs could not survive.

Yet squash at Pall Mall has become more successful at a time when squash clubs elsewhere are becoming less so. One reason is the atmosphere around the courts. 'It was always a happy place,' Jim Markwick, who joined in 1968, said. 'Everybody was very pleasant to one another. It was all very agreeable.'

Another reason is the input of Greg Pearman, the head pro at Pall Mall, who took over in 1989 to become our fourth and current professional. Arriving just 18 months after the retirement of Jack Giles, who had served the Club for some 30 years, was a daunting proposition, a bit like someone attempting to take over from the Queen Mother. Jack had been old school, charming and courteous, a pro who concentrated on giving his lessons, marking Bath Club Cup matches, stringing rackets, renewing grips and the like. No one ever had a bad word to

Head pro Greg Pearman (right) and Mark 'Sparky' Jackson, his assistant, on the balcony overlooking court one. During Greg and Mark's time, the number of Club members playing squash has risen to more than 1200.

say about him. He was even good at playing his part in the often uproarious evenings that are formally described as finals nights.

Without disregarding the influences left by Jack, Greg, 28 when he started at Pall Mall, decided the professionals had to be the engine of the squash section, generating competition for those who wanted to compete, giving lessons to those who needed coaching, and making the place approachable, lively and fun, and somewhere to drop in and have a chat before or after a game. And he has proved himself right. Greg has ignited squash at Pall Mall, made it vibrant in a way it might never have been. He gives as many as nine doubles or singles coaching lessons daily, plays members competitively when challenged and is an irrepressibly benign, smiling presence around the squash area.

Once Greg realised that ladders were not working at Pall Mall he replaced them with leagues, and suddenly the number of people wanting to play took off. 'Ladders never work, leagues do,' he said. 'Leagues have a play-by date, ladders don't. Leagues are time-based, ladders are less so. The leagues here are extremely dynamic. They call us the "squash Nazis" because if someone has not played two matches then they are out. We don't do the softly-softly approach.'

More players meant more coaches were needed, and Mark 'Sparky' Jackson, who arrived from the Isle of Man, joined to help Greg as, later, did Lauren Briggs. Mark's easy manner has won him a host of admirers among the members whom he coaches and with whom he plays, and he and Greg are so obviously compatible. 'Greg knows that I know he is the figurehead,' Mark said. 'You couldn't have two people like Greg and myself. I do the admin, he does the talking and we both do coaching. He is very, very easy to work with.'

Credit must be given, too, to Brian McGivern for the role he played in the revival of the Club in the late 1970s and 1980s, which had a knock-on effect on squash. In the mid-1980s, McGivern, who was chairman of the squash committee

> You couldn't have two people like Greg and myself. I do the admin, he does the talking and we both do coaching

before moving on to wider roles within the Club, won approval from the board of directors for a doubles court to be built at Woodcote Park. Sir Michael Edwardes and other members put their considerable enthusiasm behind the project, which by then had been expanded to embrace the installation of two courts. Construction was duly completed in 1989, which made it easier for a doubles court to be introduced at Pall Mall 15 years later. This structure has a side wall that can be moved a few feet this way or that to convert it back from a doubles-size playing area to a singles court.

Greg and Mark give 12 hours' coaching of doubles each week, over and above their singles commitments, with the effect that, and this is detailed in a later chapter, doubles has become an important part of squash at Pall Mall. If it once was an add-on there, a game played on a singles court, then now it is a strong feature, helping to attract players to the Club who might otherwise have retired from the game.

And yet to fully explain the continued success of squash at the Club, one always comes back to the intangible, to the unique atmosphere that colours every visit to the clubhouse and the whole range of activities that take place there. As an illustration, here is a paean to Pall Mall from a member: 'Then I came across the ____ and I thought, "I'll have a bit of that too." Now I use it three times each week, Monday, Wednesday and Friday. I do ____ followed by eight lengths' fairly leisurely breaststroke in the pool. I'm a lazy sod. I try to walk across Hampstead Heath on a Sunday but the Sunday papers are a great disincentive so the ____ is my only exercise. There are days when I can hardly drag myself down the stairs ... I feel sluggish and liverish. At other times I can hardly wait to get there. I'm hooked on the ____ now. I never like to miss it. When I've finished in there I have a tremendous moral uplift.' And another, from a second member: 'I enjoy ____ because it is predictable. It's like an old glove. It fits. It's familiar. I know where everything is ...'

Replace the blanks above with 'squash' or 'squash area' and you would arrive at sentiments that could easily have sprung from the lips of Pall Mall squash players. Yet the first speaker was Stanley Baxter, the actor and comedian, on the pleasures of

the gym, and the second, Michael Wynn Jones, the author and magazine editor, talking about his favourite suite. Both perfectly capture the warmth of the two areas concerned, yet both remarks could equally refer

Brian McGivern is known for his good humour and enthusiasm for squash, qualities that were evident when he joined in 1964 and have remained so during the exceptional service he has given to the Club since then. He was chairman of the Club from 1998 to 2002 before becoming a vice-president. McGivern was one of a number of members who were instrumental in helping the Club recover from the crisis of the mid-1970s.

Greg Pearman with the Club's oldest playing member, 87-year-old Edus Warren of the United States.

to squash or the squash section – such is the universal appeal of Pall Mall to the members.

Now listen to Derek Wyatt, who retired as an MP at the 2010 election: 'So when it became absolutely essential to my work to combine entertaining authors and agents with taking brisk exercise, I sought out a club with a vintage port which never ran dry, a cigar that never ended and, more importantly, accepted women on equal terms.

'Surprise, surprise, it was ridiculously hard to find a club that fitted my esoteric criteria. One secretary told me I would find the first two in heaven and all three in hell. Another suggested I might try the SDP. A third mentioned the Stewart Murray in Manhattan but that seemed a long way to go for breakfast. The Club is perfect for me. I use it on any excuse – working breakfasts, swimming, editing manuscripts, swimming, lunch, after-lunch siestas, swimming, afternoon tea, swimming, early evening drinks, meeting authors, swimming and entertaining agents. If only it was closer to my office I'd use it a lot more.'

Now this is what we want from our club, isn't it? And this is what we want from our squash club, too, isn't it? And it is because they feel the squash section provides this magical mixture that members remain members. They are happy there. They enjoy it, regardless of age. Greg's oldest pupil is 87, his most junior 80 years younger.

To me the squash section is a magnificent part of the Club, which is itself one of my favourite places in the entire world. I once decided that I could happily live in the Pall Mall clubhouse. I would play squash and swim in the basement, have my shoes cleaned

ABOVE: *The squash gallery at Pall Mall, complete with photographs of players, personalities and moments of glory from days gone by. 'The past may be a foreign country … but it is very visible in this quarter of the Royal Automobile Club.'* FACING PAGE: *The Long Bar at Pall Mall. 'Players of all ages continue to pound away on court – and make their way upstairs for a restoring drink or meal afterwards.'*

or my hair cut on the mezzanine floor, eat on the ground floor, read in the library on the first floor and stay in one of the suites. That would be heaven. I am not alone in having this love for the place. 'If I were destitute my membership of the Club is just about the last thing I would give up,' Stuart Courtney said.

Something else happened that week in October when I was visiting the Club for the first time in some months. Having spent an enjoyable half-hour watching a squash match being played downstairs, I went to the Long Bar, and for a few moments looked around the busy room. To my right, towards the billiards and snooker room, knots of people were standing at the bar talking, or sitting in leather chairs. In front of me two or three people were watching football on television. In the eating area to my left there was hardly a free seat. Even the members' table was full.

I said to myself, this is what it should be like: noisy but not deafening, cheerful and providing a service for members; somewhere for men and women to eat and drink, sit and talk and be able to watch television from time to time. If it took some time for me to realise how well the Long Bar was working that night, then it is fair to say that it had taken the Club some time to find out how to make it work.

If I were destitute my membership of the Club is just about the last thing I would give up

In a book about London clubs published in 1979, Anthony Lejeune wrote of them as follows: 'The treasures they contain and the way of life they represent, their annals and legends, surely deserve – from any point of view, historical, sociological or merely nostalgic – to be recorded with affection and respect.' No one can deny that insofar as squash at the Royal Automobile Club is concerned it is a treasure and it is being accorded affection and respect.

" Imagine how a member must have felt at the privilege of entering the magnificent clubhouse soon after it opened 100 years ago "

The First
Fifty Years

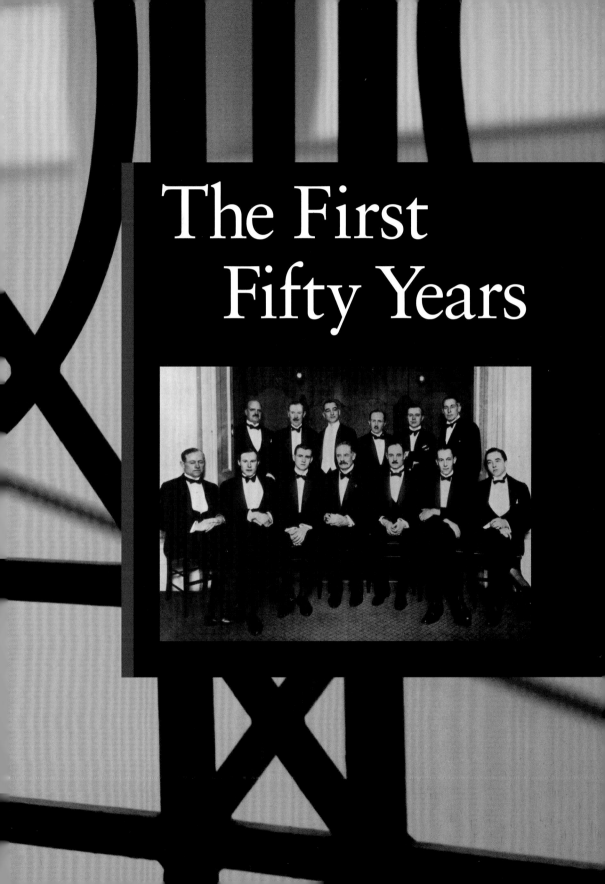

Anyone travelling along Pall Mall in 1909 would have noticed a large hole in the south side of the street. It was like 'the ruins of some mysterious earthquake', according to one newspaper. The hole, as deep as 50 feet in places, was where construction of the Pall Mall clubhouse would soon start. The building would be completed at a reported cost of £250,000 in time for the clubhouse to open its doors in March 1911. It was one of the most ambitious construction projects of the Edwardian era in London.

In 1910, when admitted for a preview, the press were said to have gasped at the splendours of engineering – the great air ducts designed to 'drive out the smog of Pall

Mall with the pure air of Carlton Terrace', the telephone exchange, the rifle range, the newspaper office and the photographic studio. Harold Catt, the Club librarian 80 years later, wrote in an historical article that 'members were already licking their lips at the luxuries that awaited them, at the same time resolving to keep them strictly for themselves. "The ladies (God bless them) are excellent in their proper place, but the premises of the [Royal Automobile Club] do not come into that category," sniffed one member.'

We are more concerned, however, with the three squash courts that were built in the basement. Squash at this time was in its infancy in London. Four courts had been built on the site of one roofless rackets court at Harrow School in 1864, and just before the end of the century it was noted that a number of Old Harrovians had built

> **There are no other clubs in central London with our facilities now, and there certainly weren't then. There was nowhere else in London quite like it**

courts at their country estates. The first courts at a London club were the two at the Queen's Club, which are said to have opened in 1905.

If you think how good it is now to be able to go to Pall Mall for a game and then a drink and perhaps supper in the Long Bar, then imagine how a member must have felt at the privilege of entering the magnificent clubhouse soon after it opened 100 years ago, descending to the squash courts and playing a game with a friend or having a lesson from Oke Johnson followed by a swim. Some say that Charles Arnold, at the Bath Club from 1911, was the first professional, as we understand the term, at a London club, but our own Oke was appointed at Pall Mall in 1910, albeit initially as real tennis pro and he did not take up his squash coaching duties until the following year. There are no other clubs in central London with our facilities now, and there certainly weren't then. There was nowhere else in London quite like it.

When the British get together and play games, it does not take long before a committee of the players is formed to run the activity, to see fair play and keep order. Sure enough, on Friday 14 June 1912 a meeting was

FACING PAGE: *Not a traffic warden in sight. The frontage of the Royal Automobile Club at 89 Pall Mall, photographed in the early years of the twentieth century.*

held at Pall Mall of the Club's 'Squash Racquet[s]' players (the Club preferred the 'racquets' spelling until 1936, when it adopted the style 'rackets'), at which a squash committee was formed. The seven members were the Hon Dudley Carleton, Col R.E.B. Crompton (one of the founder members of the Club), Dr T. Drysdale, Mr A. Mayer, Mr F.W. Polehampton, Capt H.S. Scott-Harden and Mr P. Wilkins. Scott-Harden proposed Colonel Crompton as chairman 'for the ensuing year', and Dr Drysdale, of whom a lot more will be heard, seconded him.

The committee did not hang about. The first meeting was held five days later when it was decided to try and draft some regulations to govern the play of squash. Then came the first mention of the length of time allowed for a game – half an hour on the two 'northern courts' (believed now to be courts two and three), starting on 1 July. The cost was 9d (4p) per member and 1s 6d (8p) for a guest, and these charges were doubled when play was with the professional. It was also proposed that a suggestions book be put in the changing room.

It was not many years before competitive squash got under way. Writing in the Lonsdale Library of Sports, Games & Pastimes series of books in the 1930s, John Armitage stated, 'There is literally no history of Squash results before 1920. Before that date there was little or no play in a competitive spirit and actually the first year of any consequence is 1922.' However, this statement rather overlooks the

MEETING OF SQUASH RACQUET PLAYERS.

A meeting of Squash Racquet players was held on Friday, 14th June, 1912, after dinner, when there were present: Mr. H. Blaiberg, Mr. E. B. Blobb, Col. R. E. B. Crompton, C.B., Mr. C. Crompton, the Hon. Dudley Carleton, Dr. T. Drysdale, Mr. A. Duckham, F.C.S., Mr. C. E. Hart, Mr. C. W. Lowther, Mr. A. Mayer, Mr. C. D. Rotch, Capt. H. S. Scott-Harden, Capt. T. M. Kincaid Smith, Mr. C. D. Seligman, Mr. R.B. Wimbush, Mr. P. Wilkins, and the Secretary.

A Squash Racquets Sub-Committee was formed consisting of the following gentlemen: The Hon. Dudley Carleton, Col. R.E. B. Crompton, C.B., Dr. T. Drysdale, Mr. A. Mayer, Mr. F. W. Pole-hampton, Capt. H. S. Scott-Harden, and Mr. P. Wilkins.

On the motion of Capt. H. S. Scott-Harden, seconded by Dr. T. Drysdale, it was resolved:

That Col. R. E. B. Crompton, C.B., be Chairman of the Sub-Committee for the ensuing year.

The first meeting of the Sub-Committee was fixed for Wednesday, 19th June, at 7 o'clock.

....Chairman.

Date.....................1912.

The minutes of 14 June 1912 record that Colonel Crompton was to be chairman of the Club's squash racquets committee 'for the ensuing year'. In the event, Crompton was still in the post in 1936.

The year 1922 also marked the start of the Bath Club Cup, now the longest-running inter-club squash competition in the world

fact that the Club had played a match against the Royal Academy at Woolwich before the First World War and started both its Open and its Handicap events in the 1919/20 season. Also in 1920, Charles Read defeated Oke in the first Professional Championship.

The years 1921 and 1922 brought the first men's and women's Amateur Championships, and the latter year also marked the start of the Bath Club Cup, now the longest-running inter-club squash competition in the world. The competition was inaugurated by Lord Desborough, the Earl of Kimberley and Sir John Wilson-Taylor – respectively the Bath Club's chairman, vice-chairman and secretary – as a squash tournament for West End social clubs. According to a contemporary note, 'The intention was that it should be a social event whereby squash players could play a match and then join together at dinner at which the home club would be host.' On 10 October 1922, *The Times* announced the new competition: 'A fifty-guinea challenge cup has been offered by the Bath Club for competition at squash rackets between the London clubs possessing squash courts. At present the competition will be restricted to singles matches, each club being represented by three players. Among the clubs which will take part are Lord's, Prince's, Royal Air Force, Bath and Royal Automobile Club.'

The first match was played on 1 November 1922, and the next day *The Times* reported, 'A start in the new and particularly interesting squash rackets competition was made at the Bath Club yesterday where the Bath Club beat the RAF Club by three matches to none.' By the end of the season the Club emerged the winners, the team comprising Dr Theodore Drysdale, W.F. 'Ginger' Basset (described as the fittest man in England by the magazine *Squash Rackets, Fives, Tennis and Rackets*) and Cecil Browning, an Old Harrovian who was runner-up in the 1922/23 Amateur Championship. Ginger Basset was largely instrumental in winning the trophy for his club, noted the magazine. Basset won our Open four times in all and the Handicap event twice, and would become treasurer and vice-chairman of the Squash Rackets Association. His qualities of endurance were legendary, but nothing exceeded his

Meetings were held at Pall Mall, and Walter Peasgood, who was clerk to the Club committees, took the minutes. This was the first of a series of historic events in which the Club played a leading part and is one of the reasons why it thinks of itself as the home of squash.

In February 1923 the Squash Rackets Representative Committee, meeting at Pall Mall, discussed four types of ball. The 'Standard' ball used by the Club was manufactured under licence to a specification laid down by Colonel Crompton. It was made from a top-grade red rubber, with a high-gloss, black-enamelled surface carrying the Royal Automobile Club name printed in red monogram style. The others were a large and heavy perforated ball used by the Bath Club, known as the 'holer' ball and marked 'Black all through'; an alternative ball used by the Bath Club and marked 'J. Wisden's Royal'; and a ball used by Queen's Club made by Gradidge. The first three of these balls were tested at Lord's and it was announced that the Club's 'Standard' ball would be used at the 1922/23 Amateur. Much like the issue of court size, attempts to regulate the squash ball were not wholly popular. For instance, in November 1922 *The Times*'s squash correspondent had written, 'There is a scheme on foot to standardize the squash ball, but this is, in the writer's opinion, a mistake. Squash rackets is not a standard game and can never be one.' Discussion about the squash ball continued for years, and it was not until after the formation of the Squash Rackets

Association that some progress towards producing a standard ball was made.

Nevertheless, with each passing year the Bath Club Cup went from strength to strength, adding a second division by 1929 and a third in 1930. In the years up to the Second World War a number of interesting characters represented the Royal Automobile Club in the competition. Frank Strawson, who won the Club's A Handicap event in 1924 and would become famous later for being the first chairman of the Jesters Club, played in the Bath Club Cup not only for the Club but also for Queen's Club. Strawson's middle name was Merlin, so it was no surprise that his game smacked of wizardry. He was a good enough player to reach the semi-final of the 1924/25 Amateur, some achievement considering that he was a natural right-hander who was forced to play left-handed as a result of being wounded in the First World War. Like Jim Dear, one of the old-time professionals, Strawson died on court, and in his memory the Jesters play an annual match against the governing body – initially the Squash Rackets Association, subsequently England Squash and today England Squash & Racketball (ESR).

Other names of note were D.G. Yeats Brown, who had won the Drysdale Cup in 1938; Beverley 'Bev' H. Lyon, the Gloucestershire cricket captain who once scored a century for his county after his brother Malcolm, or 'Dar', had scored a double hundred for Somerset in the

In the years up to the Second World War a number of interesting characters represented the Club in the Bath Club Cup

Table of Weights, Measurements, Bounce Tests of Squash Balls.

Ball	W Weight in Grammes	D Dia. in m/m	B Bounce % of rise to drop	P Value of P = W/D²·B	
R.A.C. standard	26	39.5	50%	100	Average of 12 measurements and bounce tests.
Wisden Royal	34	41.0	54%	142	One Ball supplied by Lord Wodehouse.
Queens Nigger	33	41.2	55%	142	One ball by Colonel Kearsey.
Bath large ball with hole	36½	42.7	59%	160	One ball by Lord Wodehouse.

Where W = Weight.
D = Diameter.
B = % of Bounce.
F = Force required at Racquet.
P = WD·B

FACING PAGE: *The Squash Rackets Representative Committee minutes of 2 February 1923 record the decision to test three types of ball for possible use in that year's Amateur.* RIGHT. *An annex to the 2 February minutes, giving details of the four types of ball discussed at the meeting.*

same match; H.B.T. 'Teddy' Wakelam, the first rugger commentator; and W.B. Scott, racing driver and Scottish rugger trialist who, in a foretaste of James Hunt 30 years later, played for the Club when he had spare time from his motor sport. He was a descendant of Sir Walter Scott and wore the great man's signet ring. There were also undoubted stars such as Amr Bey, an Egyptian diplomat who was appointed Club captain in 1934. He was spoken of with awe as the best player the game had seen to this time – but more of Amr Bey in later chapters.

Meanwhile, further changes took place in the administration of squash, again involving

FACING PAGE TOP: *The Bath Club Cup honours boards at Pall Mall, situated in the gallery above the squash courts.*
BELOW: *A photograph recording the 1925 match between England and the USA and featuring the three founding fathers of the Bath Club Cup – Lord Desborough, the Earl of Kimberley and Sir John Wilson-Taylor. Back row (left to right): Sir John Wilson-Taylor, G. Robarts (Eng), A.E. Ellis (USA), W.F. Basset (Eng), V.A. Cazalet (Eng), Earl of Kimberley. Seated: H.E. Mills (USA), W.D. Macpherson (Eng), E.M. Hinkle (USA), Lord Desborough, J.E. Palmer-Tomkinson (Eng), C.S. Clark (USA), J. de V. Keefe (USA).*
RIGHT: *The minutes of the final Club squash committee meeting before the Second World War. Among the points discussed was how the Club should honour Amr Bey on his retirement 'from official competitions'.*

SQUASH RACKETS COMMITTEE.

A meeting of this Committee was held on Thursday, 24th November, 1938, at 5 o'clock, when there were present: Col. W. F. Basset (Chairman), Major A.B.H. Bridges, O.B.E., Mr. L. H. Crispe, Mr. H.L.H. Nunn, Capt. J.B.R. Windham, Mr. F. G. Wheler, the Assistant Secretary and Clerk to Committees.

MINUTES.--The Minutes of the 14th September were read, confirmed and signed by the Chairman.

F. AMR BEY.--The Committee discussed the suggestion that Amr Bey's services to the Club should be recognised in some way as he had decided to retire from official competitions, although he would still be willing to play for the R.A.C. in Club matches. The suggestion that a informal dinner should be arranged had been mentioned to Amr Bey, who had requested that this suggestion be not adopted, and the Committee therefore decided that a letter of appreciation, signed by all the Members of the Committee, be sent to him. Approval of the letter was left to the Chairman and Major Bridges.

R.A.C. HANDICAP TOURNAMENT.--The following points were settled:

   a. The entry list to close on Wednesday, 14th December.

   b. The A Section of the Tournament to start on Monday, 19th December.

   c. The Regulations to be the same as those for the previous Tournament.

      Capt. Windham kindly undertook to allot handicaps, etc.

      The Committee thanked Capt. Windham for arranging the Open Tournament.

R.A.C. V. MIDDLESEX HOSPITAL. 23rd FEBRUARY, 1939.--Mr. Wheler undertook to act as Team Manager for this match.

OPEN AND PROFESSIONAL CHAMPIONSHIPS.--It was reported that the two matches between J. Dear (Professional Champion) and A.E. Biddle (Challenger), would be held at the R.A.C. on the 7th and 14th December.

      The Chairman reported that he had informed the two Professionals that they could practise in the morning up to 12 noon or from 2.30 to 4.30--if the Court had not been booked.

UNDER 40 AND OVER 40 MATCH.--It was reported that Mr. R.S. Dyball had kindly offered a Cup for competition in October and the Committee accepted it and agreed that a letter of thanks, signed by the Chairman or the Committee, be sent to him. Instructions were given for Mr. Dyball to be asked to specify the conditions for this competition.

Date. Dec" 1th ..... 1938.   ....Chairman.

the Club. By 1928 the Tennis & Rackets Association sub-committee could not cope with the expansion of the game. It was time a dedicated body took over, and in December of that year the Squash Rackets Association was formed, although its executive committee did not come into being until 1 April 1929. Lord Wodehouse was the SRA's first chairman; Alec Kearsey, a member of Queen's Club, was secretary; and the treasurer was Ginger Basset of the Royal Automobile Club. Committee meetings were held at Pall Mall, and Walter Peasgood continued to take the minutes until the end of the Second World War. By that time Peasgood had gone blind and was unable to continue his good work. He retired and his duties to the SRA were undertaken by Miss Coles, secretary to the Secretary of the Club, and she was briefly succeeded by members of the staff of Duncan Ferguson, the Club's auditor, who attended meetings and took minutes. This situation could not continue, however, and though the organisation continued to hold its meetings at the Club, on 1 September 1948 the SRA moved into tiny offices in the

THE

ANNUAL GENERAL MEETING

of the

SQUASH RACKETS ASSOCIATION

will be held at

5.30 p.m. on Tuesday, September the 30th, 1952

at the

Royal Automobile Club, Pall Mall, London, S.W.1.

(Those attending are asked to use the western entrance to the club)

AGENDA :

1. Apologies for absence.
2. Approval of the minutes of the last annual general meeting and consideration of any matters arising therefrom.
3. Consideration of the annual report of the executive committee.
4. Consideration of the statement of accounts and balance sheet.
5. Election of the officers of the association and confirmation of the co-opted members of the executive committee.
6. Appointment of the honorary auditors for the ensuing year.
7. Proposal to add to rule 18 (c) of the association, after the words "Individual members," the words "both amateur and professional."
8. Proposal to add to rule 5 of the association, after the words "any other racket game," the words "except lawn tennis."
9. Proposal to add to rule 20 (b) of the association the following: "Clubs and other organizations in England to which affiliation to a county association is not applicable : 3 guineas or such lesser sum as the executive committee may decide."
10. Any other business of which fourteen days' notice has been given to the secretary in writing and which the chairman considers suitable for discussion at the meeting.

H. E. Hayman, secretary.

1

LEFT: *The Squash Rackets Association moved out of Pall Mall on 1 September 1948 but continued to hold their meetings at the clubhouse for some time to come.* FACING PAGE: *The fencing salle at Pall Mall, pictured in 1911. In 1935 it was converted to what was, until 1950, the Club's only standard-size squash court.*

Haymarket, and Henry Hayman, a retired schoolmaster, became its secretary.

Another significant squash issue to be addressed at Pall Mall after the war was the need to bring the Club's courts up to the correct specification. In 1935 the fencing *salle* had been converted to a standard-size squash court, but it took a significant effort by Brian Phillips, deputy chairman of the squash committee and one of the country's leading players, to realise the conversion of the Club's three original courts. In November 1948 Phillips wrote a damning assessment of the situation. He suggested widening courts one, two and three so that each measured 21 feet across; standardising the back walls of the courts; and removing the painted teak on the floor and replacing it with strips of maple.

In trying to convince the powers that be at the Club of the importance of making these changes, Phillips wrote as follows: 'The [Club] is the leading Squash Rackets Club of Great Britain. In the past its Members have supplied the Winner of the Open and Amateur Championships in the person of F.D. Amr Bey ... They have supplied the runner-up in the Amateur Championship in the years 1923 and 1929 in the persons of C. Browning Esq. and Col. W.F. Basset. The Club has also won the Bath Club Cup on six occasions. All this has been done in spite of the lack of more than one standard court.'

Phillips talked of the embarrassment of the Club captain at seeing visitors having to

play on a non-standard court. He explained that the Club had been invited by the SRA to be the venue for the England v Scotland fixture in March 1949 and these matches would have to be played on one court. Phillips concluded: 'From all this it is hoped that the point has been clearly shown that unless the squash rackets section of the Club is made more attractive to young players then other Clubs will get the talent and the [Royal Automobile Club's] position will sink to the bottom of the third division. By the Committee's proposal something will have been put forward to maintain the [Club] in its proper position as Headquarters Squash Rackets Association [even though the SRA had moved out the previous year] and Great Britain's leading Squash Rackets Club.'

That his campaign was successful is a tribute to Phillips's personal skills, not to

Another significant squash issue to be addressed at Pall Mall after the war was the need to bring the Club's courts up to the correct specification

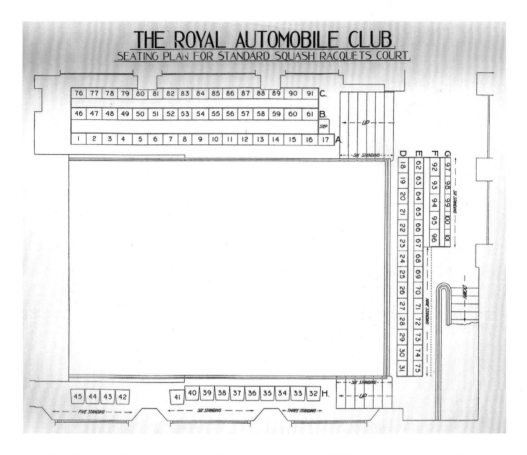

mention his standing in the game. He represented the Club in his first Bath Club Cup match on 17 January 1939, playing Neville Hooper of Queen's Club, and in all played five pre-war Bath Club Cup matches, all at first string, and countless postwar ones. Tall, intelligent, thoughtful and articulate, he was not an easy man to deny. Throughout 1949 there are reports in the minutes of meetings being held, plans being drawn up and building licences being applied for; and on 1 October 1950, work was finished. The three courts were renumbered, the best, formerly court four, becoming court one. A further court was built to fit the available remaining space and turned out to be the size of an American court. It was the only one in the country and was used by players wanting to practise for that form of the game. An exhibition match on 22 November 1950 marked the formal opening of the new courts.

The Pall Mall court improvements provided the backdrop to another golden period

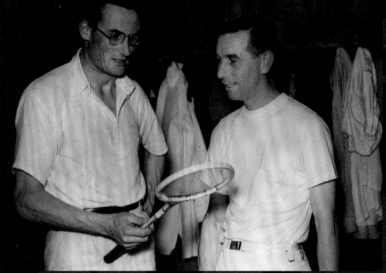

FACING PAGE: *The plan for the standard-size squash court that replaced the Pall Mall fencing salle in 1935. It is now court one, the Giles Court.*
RIGHT: *Brian Phillips (left) in conversation with Jim Dear, who lost three Open Championship finals to Amr Bey from 1936 to 1938 but went on to win the tournament in 1939 after the great man's retirement.* BELOW: *The Club's Bath Club Cup winning team 1950/51 and 1951/52. From left to right: Peter Phillips, Oke Johnson (professional), Brian Phillips (captain), G.V. Cotton (squash committee chairman), 'Pete' Hildick-Smith.*

SQUASH RACKETS MATCH.   Date *29ᵗʰ OCTOBER.*

ROYAL AUTOMOBILE CLUB v. *HURLINGHAM*

at *R.A.C*

1. *D.L. HODGSON*	(R.A.C.)	~~beat~~ lost to	*H. de B. PRIESTLEY*	*5-9 4-9 5-9*
2. *D.T. MEDWAY*	(R.A.C.)	beat ~~lost to~~	*W.D.N. VAUGHAN*	*10-8 9-7 1-9 9-7*
3. *B.E.F. CHEESMAN*	(R.A.C.)	beat ~~lost to~~	*F.R.J. CORBETT*	*10-9 9-3 3-9 10-8 9-7*
4.	(R.A.C.)	beat lost to	,	
5.	(R.A.C.)	beat lost to	,	

Result   R.A.C. *BEAT* HURLINGHAM   *2* matches   *1* matches

LEFT: *Filled in by Jack Giles, the scorecard for the Royal Automobile Club v Hurlingham Bath Club Cup match on 29 October 1958. David Vaughan (below when at Oxford University in 1950) is now a prominent Club member (and current president of the Jesters Club) but on this occasion was playing against the Club for Hurlingham.* FACING PAGE TOP LEFT: *More from the 1958/59 season. Lawrence Verney's match invitation and acceptance for the friendly between the Club and the RAF.* FACING PAGE BELOW: *Lawrence Verney, who represented Wales 44 times in the 1940s, 1950s and 1960s, speaking at Pall Mall on the occasion of the 80th anniversary of the Bath Club Cup in 2002.*

for our Bath Club Cup team. Up to the war the Club had won the cup on four occasions but never in successive seasons. That changed with the arrival at the Club of Gavin 'Pete' Hildick-Smith, a South African. With him at number one, Brian Phillips playing second and Peter Phillips, who was no relation, playing third, the Club was victorious in all ten of its matches in the 1950/51 competition, winning 27 ties out of a possible 30. From 1946 until 1953, the Club won the Bath Club Cup five times and finished runners-up twice. Not until the early 1960s and the time of Mike Oddy, Gerald Massy and Mike Corby was the Club to achieve such success again.

Though we are now long past the earliest days of squash at Pall Mall, it is worth recording the extraordinary service rendered by Colonel Crompton, the squash committee's first chairman. Appointed in June 1912 ('for the ensuing year', remember), Crompton was still in the post in 1936, by which time he was in his tenth decade, an age that is unlikely ever again to be matched by a squash committee member. In October 1936, Crompton retired, only to return for a short period a year later. He was a true Club man. In a magazine of the time, he was described as 'A founder of the Royal Automobile Club and one, if not the chief, sponsor of Squash Rackets for the club before the War, Colonel Crompton at the great age of 91 still serves on the [Royal

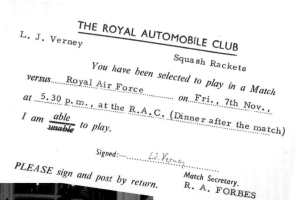

THE ROYAL AUTOMOBILE CLUB

L. J. Verney

Squash Rackets

You have been selected to play in a Match

versus.... Royal Air Force .... on Fri., 7th Nov.,

at 5.30 p.m., at the R.A.C. (Dinner after the match)

I am ~~able~~ ~~unable~~ to play.

Signed:— L.J. Verney

PLEASE sign and post by return.

Match Secretary.
R. A. FORBES

ABOVE: *Col R.E.B. Crompton, Club founder member and brilliant electrical engineer.*

Automobile Club] Squash Rackets Committee. Professionally he is known as a most distinguished soldier and engineer.' A brilliant electrical engineer, he invented the Crompton lamp, the world's first electric toaster and electric oven, and installed the lighting at Windsor Castle and King's Cross Station.

In appearance Crompton was the quintessential English sporting figure. He had silvery hair and a moustache that spread way past his mouth and out towards his cheekbones. Pictures do not reveal his height and bearing, but one can assume that he was tall and carried himself well. Colonel Crompton's longevity and contributions to the Club have an echo in the length of service of our professionals (see Chapter Four).

The year 1960 is an appropriate point to end this chapter. The Club appeared to be healthy and on a financially sound footing as it approached the end of its first half-century. Who was to know of the troubles that lay ahead, or of the surge of interest in squash that was to begin?

Who was to know of the troubles that lay ahead, or of the surge of interest in squash that was to begin?

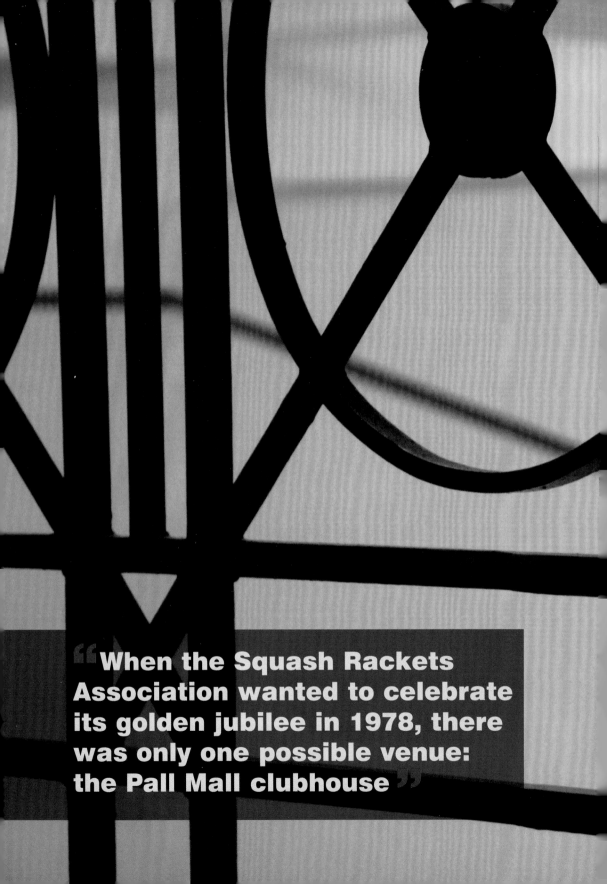

"When the Squash Rackets Association wanted to celebrate its golden jubilee in 1978, there was only one possible venue: the Pall Mall clubhouse"

Since
the Sixties

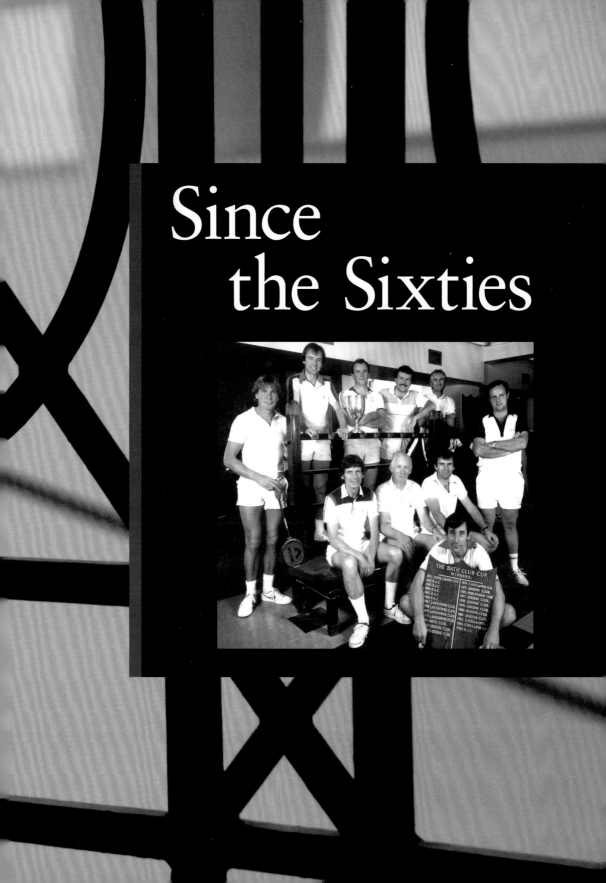

FACING PAGE: *Mike Corby (front), pictured at the team event of the 1971 World Amateur Championship with (left to right) Philip Ayton, John Easter, Peter Chalk and Paul Millman.*

In the 1960s the standard of squash at the Club was perhaps higher than ever. The leading player was Mike Oddy, who won the Drysdale in 1955/56 and the Amateur in 1960/61 and 1961/62. Then there was Mike Corby, who had won the Drysdale three years after Oddy, would win the Amateur Plate and would be beaten by Jonah Barrington in the Amateur finals of 1967/68 and 1968/69. The third member of an outstanding trio was Gerald Massy, described by Corby as 'a nuggety Old Harrovian'.

Nigel Faulks also played in the Club's Bath Club Cup team and would later captain it, and probably would have played for England but for his decision to emigrate to Iran in 1968. David Brazier was a British international who became frustrated at not being selected for the Bath Club Cup teams and went off to the Bath Club. Nigel Broomfield made occasional forays back to the Club from his Army duties.

With members such as these forming the core of its Bath Club Cup teams, it is not surprising that the Club won the competition five years in succession starting in 1962, a feat no other club had achieved up to then. The Royal Automobile Club's golden era in the competition ended in 1966, and it was 1984, when we won both Division I and Division II, before the Club next had something to celebrate in the Bath Club Cup.

'Oddy was a tall Scot,' Corby said. 'He practised and practised. He would play with Azam at the New Grampians club as many as three times each week. He hit the ball with great pace to an immaculate length again and again and again. He was the outstanding British player of his generation and he did it all on only one kidney.'

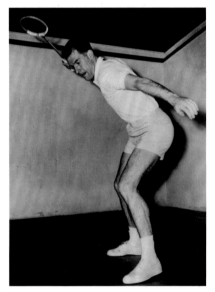

Mike Oddy of Scotland, who won the Amateur in 1960/61 and 1961/62 and was runner-up in the 1963/64 British Open, was the cornerstone of the Bath Club Cup team that carried all before it in the first half of the 1960s.

Sadly Massy was killed in September 1966 in a plane crash in the north of England. 'Gerald kept going for ever,' Faulks recalled. 'He had thighs like tree trunks. He was a rackets player who hit the ball very fluently but he was not that tight a player and that is how I beat him in the semi-final of the 1966 Open tournament after being 8-0

down in the fifth. I was understandably chuffed with myself. Three weeks later I beat Corby in the final.'

Corby was a broker at Lloyd's, like Massy, whom he had seen the day before the latter's fatal accident. A colourful character, Corby was a squash and hockey international, but with a tendency to get into trouble. He was selected to travel to Australia to represent Britain in the 1967 World Amateur Championship with Jonah Barrington, Peter Stokes and David Brazier, and the Club gave him £500 to put into a kitty to cover expenses. After competing in Australia, the British team was invited to go on and make an unofficial visit to New Zealand. Corby agreed reluctantly because he had to return to work in Britain. Once in New Zealand, he found that the host nation was weaker at squash than had been realised. Barrington decided he would play both first and second string. This meant Corby was third string and Brazier fourth. 'I was number one in England, Jonah was third or fourth in the world and I was about fifth,' Corby said. 'Frankly I found it offensive to have to play third with Jonah playing one and two.'

Corby and Brazier left New Zealand after a week and returned home to a considerable furore because it was felt they had not completed their trip and fulfilled their responsibilities as representatives of Great Britain and the SRA. As a result, Corby was banned from SRA events. This decision meant he was unable to captain our Bath Club Cup team and Faulks took it over. After a meeting with Eddie Daniel, the squash committee chairman, Corby resigned from the Club.

There is also a famous story of Corby arriving tieless at Pall Mall to play in the 1969/70 Amateur. Quinn, the imposing hall porter, tried to stop him entering the Club, but Corby evaded him by running down the steps to the squash courts. When he thought that Quinn, who had come down in the lift, was about to catch up with him, he ran up the steps again. And so on. All this made a wonderful story for Rex Bellamy, the squash and tennis correspondent of *The Times*, and it duly appeared in the paper. That did not please the Club's elders and after complaints were made to the SRA, Corby had to play his remaining matches in the Amateur at the Junior Carlton Club on the other side of Pall Mall. When Corby was allowed back in to the Club, he made his point rather neatly. He took to the court wearing a white silk tie.

When he thought that Quinn, who had come down in the lift, was about to catch up with him, he ran up the steps again

From about this time, the late 1960s, some relatively new members joined the squash committee, little realising that their names would become more involved with Club activities over the coming years. Brian McGivern and I were co-opted at the same time in 1969, as a result of a letter from Neale Stainton asking for more representatives on the committee from among members who played regularly. Chris Orriss and Peter Trimingham joined in 1974.

While McGivern's spell as chairman was still a few years away when we first joined the squash committee, mine as Bath Club Cup captain began in September 1970 after Michael Cardew had relinquished the captaincy because he had to go abroad and Nigel Broomfield had said that he too was unavailable. By 1973, however, Eddie Daniel, the fifth squash committee chairman, had fallen ill and McGivern became acting chairman, and later chairman after Daniel's death. When McGivern took on extra duties connected with the running of the clubhouse after the Club had been threatened with closure on health and safety grounds in the mid-1970s, Chris Campbell took over the chair of the squash committee.

Campbell was a knowledgeable and respected figure in squash, an exponent of the reverse-angle stroke, which won him many points. He represented Scotland on nine occasions, in 1952 becoming the first Scot to win a match in the annual Scotland v England game. He was also a member of the Club's winning Bath Club Cup team of

1953/54. Honorary treasurer of the SRA and the Jesters, Campbell was a warm-hearted host at his home near Chichester, where he had a wine cellar of enviable quality and vintage, as well as a squash court.

To me he seemed a romantic figure. I thought he resembled David Niven, and it wasn't just that he had a narrow moustache. When he put a cigarette into his cigarette holder and clenched it between his teeth while talking about his flat in Half Moon Street (or 'Half Mooners', as he called it) and holding a pink gin (a 'pinkers') in his hand, he looked and sounded more like Niven than ever. Almost all my life my nickname has been 'Hoppy', as has my father's, my son's and my aunt's. For some reason Campbell preferred something else. 'Now then, Hoppo,' he would say as he stood at the bar, the genial, charming host. 'What'll you have?'

Chris Campbell, a Scotland international in the 1950s, a Bath Club Cup winner in 1953/54 and chairman of the Club's squash committee for a year in the late 1970s.

Campbell sat as chairman of the squash committee for one year before handing the hot potato to me, though he remained a committee member until 1988. He died on 20 March 1990, aged 73.

I did not have great aims when I took over the chairmanship. Keep the ship on a steady course, I thought. Nonetheless there are certain aspects of my chairmanship upon which I look back more favourably than others. Just after I became chairman, I was shocked to receive a letter from Jack Giles asking for a rise. He said he had not had one for eight years. I am glad to say we arranged that not long after.

Nevertheless, when the Squash Rackets Association wanted to celebrate its golden jubilee in 1978, there was only one possible venue, given all that had happened there a half-century earlier: the Pall Mall clubhouse. HRH the Duke of Edinburgh, patron of the SRA, was the chief guest, and before dinner he was introduced to many of the past winners of the Amateur Championship: Dugald Macpherson (1925 and 1929), Norman Borrett (1947 to 1951), Alan Fairbairn (1953 and 1954), Roy Wilson (1955), Nigel Broomfield (1958 and 1959), Mike Oddy (1961 and 1962) and Jonah Barrington (1967 to 1969). The patron then met the three British winners of the Amateur (Closed) Championship: Jonny Leslie (1975 and 1977), Philip Ayton (1976) and Philip Kenyon (1978). Of these former champions, Oddy and Broomfield were Club members; Leslie was about to become one.

Incidentally, 25 years later, in 2003, the SRA chose the Club as the venue for its 75th anniversary celebration. Once again the Duke of Edinburgh attended, and at a reception before dinner certain

ABOVE: *A bevy of winners of the Amateur Championship and the Amateur (Closed) Championship at the SRA Golden Jubilee dinner at Pall Mall in 1978. From left to right: Philip Kenyon, Jonny Leslie, Philip Ayton, Jonah Barrington, Mike Oddy, Nigel Broomfield, Roy Wilson, Alan Fairbairn, Norman Borrett and Dugald Macpherson.*
LEFT: *HRH the Duke of Edinburgh speaks to Nigel Broomfield at the SRA Golden Jubilee dinner, as Mike Oddy (left) looks on.*

guests were presented to the patron by Mike Corby, then president of the SRA. I was talking to friends when I was nudged in the back and told to prepare myself. 'This is John Hopkins, Sir,' Corby said to Prince Philip. 'He played a bit of squash and writes about it from time to time.' 'Huh,' snorted the duke. 'That's a first. A journalist who knows what he is talking about.' 'That's a bit below the belt, Sir, if I may say so,' I said. 'Not half as below the belt as half the things that have been said about me,' replied Prince Philip.

By 1979 the SRA, which had been casting covetous glances at the Drysdale Cup, had taken over its organisation. There was a certain inevitability about this development, the Club having been finding it harder and harder to stage the event. Indeed after the 1976/77 Junior Evans boys under 16 tournament at the Club, when there had been a shortage of markers, it was made a condition of future entry that all competitors should be prepared to mark or referee matches in the early rounds.

Despite the turmoil of the times, the Club did not succumb to introspection. A team from Pall Mall competed in the Greek Open in the late 1970s, and two tours were undertaken in the 1980s to Canada, where more doubles was played than in Britain, and these trips contributed to the upsurge in interest in this form of the game.

Even so, the mood in the squash area mirrored the slightly uncertain, slightly austere attitude that existed elsewhere as the Club sought to recover completely from the troubles of the 1970s. The annual squash dinners, though, were quite lively affairs – one rather too lively. 'Nothing will be thrown tonight,' Neale Stainton said at the start of the meal and was greeted by a hail of bread rolls. Some of these ricocheted around the room, doing considerable collateral damage to wine glasses, which in

'What had been a buffet restaurant was turned into the reception area for the squash courts, with the door to the gym on the right' – just one of the many physical changes made at Pall Mall from the 1970s to the mid-1990s.

turn emptied their contents over members' shirts. Fish flew across the room, too, hitting some of the portraits. The next morning the squash committee chairman was told off in no uncertain fashion by the Club management. I know because I was that chairman.

This episode, though, was nothing compared with what had been going on, and maybe still was, in other parts of clubland. A member of one establishment, accused of having thrown a boar's head that knocked a peer of the realm senseless in the fireplace, protested his innocence. 'Not me,' the member said vigorously. 'I've thrown nothing but jelly all evening.'

The 1970s to the mid-1990s was a time of considerable physical change at both Pall Mall and Woodcote Park as the Club sought to right itself, which it did with spectacular success. At Pall Mall not only were more bedrooms added but the sports area was significantly upgraded, with a lot of money going into the refurbishment of the Turkish bath. The squash pro was given a shop inside the squash changing room for a while, its door bearing the legend 'Jack Giles MBE'. Then that door into the changing room was bricked up and what had been a buffet restaurant was turned into the reception area for the squash courts, with the door to the gym on the right. The gym itself was installed behind the courts, in what once had been the rifle range and also for a time had served as Jack's cubbyhole office.

Annual Squash Dinner
following
The Club Squash Finals
which commence at 5.30 p.m.
on
Wednesday 19th April 1989

Lounge Suit   *9 p.m. approx.*

The annual squash dinners that follow finals nights have long been lively, often uproarious, events. They remained so even during times of uncertainty and austerity at the Club, which thankfully had passed by 1989.

Dozens of other alterations were made to the clubhouse down the years. For example, the days when the bedrooms were heated by tiny gas fires into which 6d (3p) had to be inserted to gain any kind of warmth passed into history, as did the bar at the bottom of the steps overlooking the swimming pool where Robert Coote, the actor, always seemed to be having a drink. Another institution that disappeared was the man in morning dress who used to shuffle in every hour and move the newspapers around on the table in the Smoking Room.

The squash area benefited greatly from the structural changes, becoming the comfortable and commodious place it is today. Yet there was a price to pay and that was that the squash changing room became much sought after, particularly by other members – the swimmers, the sub-aqua enthusiasts, the gym users. In fact almost anybody who was not allowed to change in the squash changing room cast envious glances in its direction. 'Why do squash players get such luxurious quarters?' was their cry. Peter Trimingham, who took over from me as chairman in 1995, had to fight off suggestions from the management that there should be one big changing room for all the sports activities at Pall Mall. Trimingham battled these proposals tooth and nail, and eventually won. There was also a suggestion that court four could serve as a multipurpose space, its use divided between squash and aerobics classes, for example – an echo of a suggestion made decades earlier that an indoor golf net be erected here. After court four became the doubles court, the management decided that occasional aerobics classes could be held on it, though no longer at peak times.

Meanwhile, an era had come to an end in the squash area with the retirement in 1987 of Jack Giles, which sent the squash committee out in search of a new pro. Kevin Lewis was Jack's immediate successor, but he lasted barely 18 months before he resigned. Appointing Greg Pearman, Kevin's replacement, could arguably be one of the best moves the squash committee made in the whole of my time as chairman. He has a winning way about him and with the help of Mark Jackson and Lauren Briggs does a lot of coaching, singles and doubles. He has become exactly what we wanted when we hired him: a respected teaching pro, a man good with people who is keen to make squash at the Club ever more lively. And he is succeeding.

A mention must be made here of those men who have worked in the squash area and served us so well down the years. Contemporary records give little clue as to who they were, but Sid Johnson, for one, was held in such regard that after he died in 1961 a collection among members raised £150 for his widow – quite a sum considering that the average price of a house at that time was a little over £2000.

Sid was the first of a line of men who were all sticklers for the rules. After him came Rocky

Peter Trimingham, chairman of the squash committee from 1995 to 2004, on tour with the Club in Johannesburg, 2007.

and Davy. 'I was in awe of Rocky,' Peter Trimingham recalled. 'I was a junior sports member playing squash in the holidays and knew that if I came out of the shower with so much as a drop of water falling onto the floor, I'd be for it. He made it clear that he was the king of the changing room and frankly we could do with more of that sort of discipline today.'

My memory of Davy is of a man of medium height who had his hair plastered

down with brilliantine and always wore the sort of white jacket seen at old-fashioned men's hairdressers. He was busy and bossy but kindly, a soft heart beneath an iron exterior. The first time I had a lesson from Jack Giles, Davy took me to one side as I was digging around in my pocket to pay for it and said, 'Mr Giles would like a Guinness after his game.' This, I realised, was his way of saying I should add another 2s 6d (13p) to the court fee and the pro's fee.

Chris Orriss (left) and Tim Jenkins, the Club's first and second team captains respectively, with the Bath Club Cup at the end of the 1983/84 campaign. The Royal Automobile Club won the first and second divisions that season.

Manuel Garcia started work at the Club in 1965 and his first job was cleaning the staff changing room. Within a year he had been moved to the sports area and had become sports area supervisor by the time he retired in 1992 to return to his native Spain. It was calculated that in a typical day he served 200 swimmers, 70 visitors to the Turkish bath, 100 gym users and 150 squash players. 'A satisfied member might note that he continues the tradition of impeccable politeness that has been a hallmark of custodians of the swimming pool area in recent memory,' ran a valedictory note in *Pell-Mell & Woodcote*. Noel Davis was one of Manuel's colleagues, a man with a slightly grave face that could burst into a radiant smile, and he treated some of us to that smile for nigh on 30 years. Anwar was another of whom we have fond memories.

Gustav Ferrier became a popular figure when he worked in the squash courts for a few years early in the 2000s. 'He followed instructions to the letter,' Greg Pearman said. 'He was very, very good on the all-white rule for example and if he saw someone heading towards the courts in marking shoes he would be on to them straightaway. He

ABOVE: *The Club's Bath Club Cup winning teams in 1983/84. Back row (left to right): James Hunt, Chris Orriss, Tim Jenkins, Stuart Courtney, Peter Armstrong, David Weston. Seated: Peter Chalk, Mike Breckon, John Lloyd, John Hopkins (with honours board).* RIGHT: *Almost 20 years on, some familiar faces are among the Royal Automobile Club Veterans celebrating Bath Club Cup success in 2001/02. From left to right: Peter Trimingham, Paul Ventham, Andrew Morton, Chris Orriss, Malcolm Lees, Andrew Lowenthal, Stuart Courtney and Simon Lambert.*

was also a huge Elvis Presley fan and knew everything there was to know about Elvis. It was nice to see the way the members embraced him for what he was.'

The presiding presence now is that of Herbert 'Herbie' Washaya, who comes from Zimbabwe and first worked at the Club in the laundry while he was a student towards the end of the 1970s. When a vacancy arose in 1981, Manuel telephoned him and asked him to apply for it. From that day in 1981 to now, Herbie has continued the tradition of providing members with excellent service and does it with grace and a smile that is every bit as effervescent as was Noel's.

Keith Bush (right), who won both the Open and the A Handicap in 1988, and Andrew Lowenthal slug it out on finals night 2009.

Broadly speaking, there are three groups of players at Pall Mall: the early risers, those who race to the Club at lunchtime to squeeze in a game or can play in the mornings or afternoons, and the evening crowd. An entertaining picture of the early-morning group was provided by Harris Raphael, who wrote the following in 1985 about his fellow early-morning risers and squash players: 'There are those ... who turn up every morning regardless of traumas, personal disasters or Acts of God which mitigate against attendance ... with religious fervour these Ayatollahs of the squash courts come by car, bus, train, bicycle and even foot. Some are in their kit when they arrive; others ... come fully attired for the office merely to strip off half an hour after they got dressed. Some have odd socks or forget their pants, tie, shirt, wig or worse ...'

Morning, afternoon and evening, some 1200 members, including a growing group of women enthusiasts, now play squash at the Club. Keith Bush, a doctor with rooms in Harley Street, joined in 1986 and won the Open and A Handicap events in the same year, 1988. Only four men had done that before – Ginger Basset in 1925, Amr Bey in 1931, Mike Corby in 1961 and Stephen Jones in 1986. Ali Ispahani played at and for the Club, starting in 1976. Ispahani was a smiling Indian whose family empire

ABOVE: *Frank Watts, a member and keen squash player since 1968.* ABOVE CENTRE: *A smiling Jeremy Krzystyniak with spoils at the 2005 annual squash dinner.* ABOVE RIGHT: *Gary Mitchell, a member for almost 30 years, on finals night 2005.* BELOW: *Moving business closer to pleasure. Johnny Plumbe (left) and Andrew Morton, who relocated their firm so they could be nearer the Pall Mall squash courts.*

extended halfway round the world and almost certainly supplied tea to the Club. Mike Corby referred to him as the 'Shah of Shoreditch'.

Darren Johnson, a popular man and very talented player, had the misfortune to snap an Achilles tendon early in the Open final of 2006.

Jeremy Krzystyniak, 38, clearly has an enormous appetite for squash. He captains and plays in the Bath Club Cup second team in the winter as well as turning out for the Club's Surrey Cup team, based at Woodcote Park, in the summer.

The ebullient Frank Watts has been a member and keen player since joining the Club in 1968, and for a time in the 1980s won the doubles event with Chris Orriss every other year and five times in all. Gary Mitchell, a member since 1982, won the Wilding Trophy for the A Handicap three out of four years starting in 1990 and reached the final of the Open more than once. Johnny Plumbe first started playing squash at the Club in the mid-1980s, and he and Andrew Morton would take on Greg at lunchtime, two against one. Plumbe and Morton became so keen on squash they even moved the offices of their shipping company from Albemarle Street to Pall Mall in order to be nearer the Club.

The Squash Gallery

The Pall Mall squash section owes a great deal of its success and atmosphere to an enthusiastic and convivial membership. Here and on pages 92–93 are selections of photographs mainly from the finals nights of the 2000s, showing just some of the people who ensure that squash continues to thrive at the Club.

THIS PAGE: 1 Brothers Ben (left) and Rupert Grose with Victor Chung and Paul Ventham, 2004; 2 Meenal Devani and Dominic Wright, 2007; 3 Stephen Welton, 2009; 4 Greg Lamond, 2007; 5 David Esser, 2004; 6 Richard Winter (left), David Fell and James Gardner, 2010.

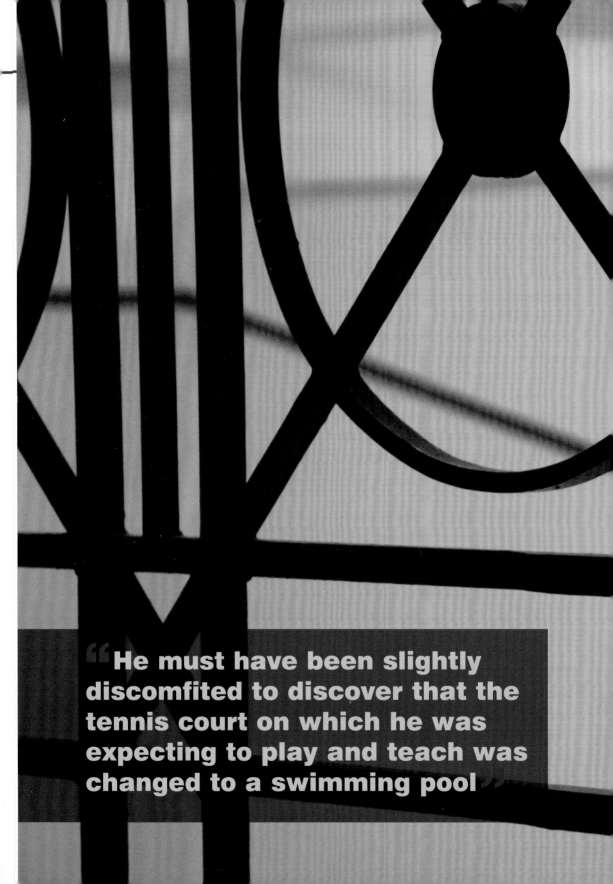

"He must have been slightly discomfited to discover that the tennis court on which he was expecting to play and teach was changed to a swimming pool

The Professionals

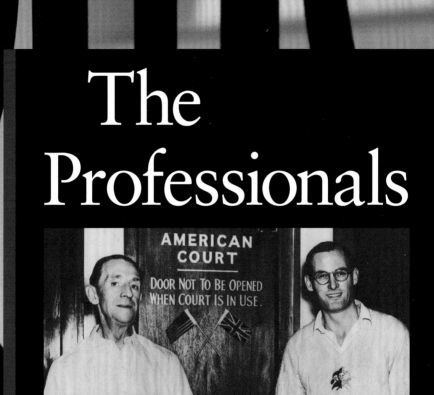

There must be something about the relationship between the Club and its professionals that breeds longevity because Oke Johnson and his successors have a tradition of serving us well and long. Oke was our pro for 45 years, Jack Giles, who followed Oke, stayed for 31 years and Greg Pearman, who joined the Club in 1989, remains here to this day. That Kevin Lewis was with us for barely 18 months, after Jack and before Greg, is the exception.

To get the full measure of the fact that we have had only four squash pros since Oke was appointed in 1910, consider this: during that time there have been the same number of pros at Pall Mall as there have been monarchs on the British throne. George V was king from 1910 until 1936. George VI came to the throne in 1936 and reigned until 1952 whereupon Her Majesty Queen Elizabeth II acceded, and she remains as sovereign nearly 60 years later. Between George V and George VI, Edward VIII was briefly king, his reign of just under one year not that much shorter than Kevin Lewis's tenure as Pall Mall professional. In effect, then, since 1910 there have been three monarchs on the British throne and three pros at Pall Mall. In the same period 19 people have been prime minister, and

BELOW: *The magnificent swimming pool at Pall Mall, with its mosaics and Sicilian marble columns, occupies the space set aside for a real tennis court in the original clubhouse building plans.* FACING PAGE: *Initially taken on as real tennis professional before the clubhouse opened its doors in 1911, Oke Johnson instead taught squash at Pall Mall for 45 years.*

several of these, including Stanley Baldwin and Winston Churchill, have held the office more than once. While the world has witnessed the change from the hansom cab and penny post to private jet and cyberspace, the needs of our squash-playing members have been attended to, in the main, by only Oke, Jack, Kevin and Greg. Remarkable.

Since 1910 there have been the same number of pros at Pall Mall as there have been monarchs on the British throne

Oke Johnson

Where would the interview have taken place? Where would the elders of the Royal Automobile Club have taken the quiet young man who wanted to become the Club's tennis professional to have a formal chat with him? The meeting could not have been at the Pall Mall building because in 1910 the clubhouse had yet to open its doors.

So where did it occur? Was it at one of the addresses in Piccadilly or Dover Street that the Club used before moving to Pall Mall? Or perhaps there was no interview at all. Maybe Ariel William Bedwin Johnson was never required to put on whites and go through his paces as were some of his successors as squash professional.

This is quite likely in fact because 'Oke', as he was known, was engaged as a real tennis professional. He must have been slightly discomfited to discover that the tennis court on which he was expecting to play and teach was changed to a swimming pool before the building opened and before he could hit a single stroke. Thus it was that Oke Johnson became not the first tennis professional at the Club but the first squash professional. He remained at Pall Mall until 1956, dying in harness. To have given service for almost a half-century is devotion of an unusual kind, and one hopes that Oke was as happy at the end as he had been when he started the job.

Back in 1912, the first minutes of the squash committee reveal that a junior pro was engaged to help Oke 'in playing with Members, and to assist in the General Dressing Room'. While it may be incidentally surprising that a squash committee had not been formed immediately the Club opened the previous year, these minutes confirm that the current assistants, Mark Jackson and Lauren Briggs, who work with Greg Pearman, are not the Club's first such employees, not by a cool 90 or so years.

Did something subsequently happen to the relationship between Oke and the Club around the time of the outbreak of the First World War? Did Oke have to resign in order to go and fight for King and Country? It rather sounds as though he did because at the first committee meeting after the war, on 5 March 1919, the minutes tell us that a report would be made to the committee to include the circumstances of Oke's leaving the Club and his postwar demobilisation. The returning Oke was to be given a three-month trial alongside a man named Stevens. Who was Stevens? Though we do not know, we can surmise that he was the man who took Oke's duties while Oke was away at the war. Perhaps Stevens was the 'junior pro' referred to as long ago as 1912, who had presumably worked alongside Oke and then soldiered on single-handedly. In other words, Stevens was the incumbent when Oke came back.

Yet if there had been two professionals

The minutes of the June 1912 squash committee meeting that allowed for a junior professional to be engaged to assist Oke Johnson. Was this junior pro the mysterious Stevens whom Oke replaced after the First World War?

before the war, why could there not be two after the war? Was it the economics of postwar Britain, perhaps? Anyway it led the committee to consider the merits of both men, and this worked in Oke's favour. He got his job back, and Stevens was given one month's earnings in lieu of notice.

We do not know how much the squash pros earned then but can assume that the words 'king's ransom' would never be appended to any description of their salaries. In 1922, for example, Oke was awarded a rise of £1 per week. What we do know is that Oke's income was supplemented by matches against other professionals. For example, he and Charles Read of Queen's Club played for the Professional Championship of the British Isles on a home and away basis, £200 going to the winner, a remarkable figure for those days. Oke played Read twice, in 1920 and 1928. In 1920 he lost in straight games (15-8, 15-2, 15-5) at Queen's but won at the Club (12-15, 15-9, 15-3, 15-10). Eight years later the pattern was the same, Read winning at Queen's (9-1, 9-0, 9-2; note the change in the scoring method) and Oke winning at Pall Mall (9-6, 3-9, 10-8, 2-9, 9-4). Thus though Read won on aggregate, Oke kept his record of never having been beaten on his home courts, which he maintained to the end.

> **Thus though Read won on aggregate, Oke kept his record of never having been beaten on his home courts, which he maintained to the end**

While there is also talk of his having played matches against the pro at Wellington College and against Charles Arnold at the Bath Club, little more is known of Oke, or 'Johnnie' as he was called by some members. Research reveals photographs of him, showing him to be about six feet tall with a rather distinctive habit of turning his head slightly to the left when being photographed, as though to present his better side to the camera. He was slim, with black hair that receded rather more slowly as the years went by than that of many others and, according to Brian Phillips, he had 'unmistakeable Dorset tones'. These tones were heard when he called out in games he was marking, 'Eight-all. Anybody's game.' There is in the squash court gallery a photograph of him and Phillips standing outside the American Court. Oke is wearing a short-sleeved shirt, and his trousers are held up by a webbed belt.

Oke gave lessons and played all-comers, and while he was not as good a player as either Jack Giles or Greg Pearman, on the rickety courts at Pall Mall he was a match for anyone. He had an endearing way about him. He was no sergeant-major on court, preferring instead to talk quietly to his pupils. Undoubtedly his most successful was Abdel Fattah Amr – more widely known as F.D. Amr Bey, or just Amr Bey – who came to England with the Egyptian Davis Cup tennis team in 1928, aged 18, and returned later that year as a diplomat. Amr Bey duly joined the Club and played regularly with Oke. His rapid progression from a raw young man of undoubted talent into one of the world's best of his time and, indeed, one of the greatest of all squash players took only a few years.

'At the [Royal Automobile Club] Amr Bey met his Svengali – Oke Johnson,' Phillips wrote in 1978. 'Under Oke's tutelage Amr's natural talents were perfected and Amr added five British Open championships and six Amateur championships to the ten consecutive [Club] Open championships he won while a member. One Club hopeful who drew Amr in the first round of the Club championship was heard to remark he did not think his case absolutely hopeless as "Amr might break a leg you know." "Yes," Oke replied overhearing this. "But it's extremely unlikely he will break both."'

In 1952 Oke watched Nigel Broomfield, a precocious young man of 14, win his first Drysdale Cup, the competition for boys under the age of 19. Broomfield had grown up near squash courts at Catterick Camp in Yorkshire and whenever he was bored he would take himself off to have a hit. He went on to win the Drysdale Cup on two more occasions and the Amateur Championship in 1958 and 1959.

Broomfield recalled a conversation with Oke that affected the way he played squash – even if not for a few years. 'I was young and winning tournaments and like all teenagers I thought the game was easy,' Broomfield said. 'I moved around the court hitting the ball as hard and enthusiastically as I could until it wasn't hit back to me.

'Oke saw me and watched me and goodness knows what he thought of this young rather beefy teenager. He said to me, "You've got the fast game, clearly. But have you got a slow game? What about learning to mix it up? Have you thought about what you do when you get into trouble, when you want to take a breather or if your opponent

Oke (left) and Brian Phillips, then captain of the Bath Club Cup team, at the opening of the American Court in 1950. The court came into being as a result of reconstruction begun at the end of the 1940s. It no longer exists as such; the area is now taken up by the doubles court.

keeps on returning your shots? Can you slow it down a bit?" His main message was that you can't play one-paced squash.

'I looked at him as a 14-year-old would and thought to myself, "What on earth are you talking about, you old man? What can you possibly teach me?" It turned out Oke could teach me a lot. He was not doddery. He would go on court with members and have a knock-around but he wouldn't have been able to do a 30- or 40-minute game. He was a kind, gentle man. He used to mark games from the gallery. He said things to me with humour. We went on court together and he showed me what to do, how to slow the game down, how to move to the front of the court. "Now here is one type of lob, here is another and here is a third," he said before tossing the ball to me for me to have a go.

'The realisation of what he was saying took time to sink in. In fact it wasn't until I played [Ibrahim] Amin in the final of the 1959 Amateur, at Pall Mall actually. I was rather less fit than I would have liked because I was in the midst of my basic Army training and used to being shouted at by sergeant-majors. I was not playing much squash and was therefore not squash fit. The previous year I had been up at Cambridge, was playing a bit of rugby to a half-decent standard and I was fit. I didn't lose a game on my way to winning that year's Amateur held at the Lansdowne.

'But in 1959 the Bruce Court at the Lansdowne was out of action for some reason that I do not remember so the Amateur was held at Pall Mall. In the final again against Amin there came a time when I suddenly found myself running out of petrol so I threw in two or three cross-court drops to get Amin from behind the T, which is where he had worked out he needed to be to return my shots. I took the pace off the game. I made him move. That's when Oke's lesson hit home. I went on to win 3-1 but there were moments when it was a damned close-run thing.'

Broomfield was to be Oke's last top-class pupil. Oke was taken ill on court on 18 January 1956 and died four days later.

Jack Giles

Even before his sudden and untimely death intervened, Oke's retirement from his post as pro at Pall Mall had been anticipated, and plans were laid to try and lure Jack Giles to the Club from Abbeydale Squash Club in Sheffield, where he was the teaching pro.

Chris Campbell, then a member of the Royal Automobile Club's squash committee, was deputed to go to Sheffield and recruit Jack. Campbell was well suited to such a task. He was treasurer of the Squash Rackets Association and chairman of the pros' committee. He knew Jack, as well as Jack's brother Bob, and had played rackets with their father. Campbell was also a referee of some note and would go on to referee many matches in partnership with Jack.

LEFT: *A caricature of Jack Giles, who succeeded Oke Johnson at Pall Mall and served the Club from 1956 until his retirement in 1987.* FACING PAGE: *Jack plays a forehand against his great friend Hashim Khan in the final of the 1977/78 British Open Vintage competition, which Hashim eventually won.*

'I failed,' Campbell reported. 'Jack being a man of integrity refused to discuss matters while Oke was still employed by the Club.' But when Oke died, there was no longer any reason for

Jack not to move south and he duly did so, starting at Pall Mall in February 1956 when he was 35.

Jack had a distinguished career as a competitive player. In 1946 he had been runner-up in the RAF Championship, and starting in 1954 he won the Professional Championship of the United Kingdom a record ten successive times before retiring undefeated. He represented the Professionals in more matches than did any of his colleagues, playing 18 times in all, 15 in a row. He also set up coaching schemes in Sweden, gave exhibitions and organised courses for referees and markers. At various times he coached both the British men's and women's teams.

It was one of Jack's claims that in a half-century of driving he had never had an accident, and he was almost as proud of this as he was of another unusual achievement – that in his competitive career he had never conceded a penalty point. Alex Fynn, the sports consultant, was reminded of how keenly Jack felt about this when they played together one day in the early 1980s.

'I had been let down by an opponent and decided for the one and only time to pay and asked Jack for a game. I was then in my thirties, Jack was in his sixties. I ought to point out that I had played sport to a reasonable level and that inculcated in me a degree of gamesmanship. We started playing and fairly early on I felt he was in the way and asked for a let.

'Well! Jack looked at me. He wasn't angry but he was peeved. "I've heard about you and your calling for lets," he said, "but I didn't believe it. Now I've seen it with my own eyes. The last person who

Starting in 1954 he won the Professional Championship of the United Kingdom a record ten successive times before retiring undefeated

LEFT: *Jack Giles photographed at the Squash Rackets Association's 50th Anniversary dinner, held at Pall Mall in 1978.* FACING PAGE: *Jack Giles on the court that bears his name. Formerly court one, the Jack Giles Court has been so called since 1986.*

asked for a let against me was in the British Professional Championships of 1947 and he didn't get one either!"'

Jack formed a strong and lasting friendship with Hashim Khan, which informed his life. When Hashim first came to Britain in 1951, he and Jack got to know one another quickly and well. Hashim found Jack to be charming and an elegant player, who was rarely ruffled. Jack found Hashim to be hugely better than he. In *The History of Squash Rackets*, John Horry, who was secretary of the SRA from 1955 to 1972, wrote: 'Hashim … has many claims to be considered as the greatest player the game has so far seen … But as a strokemaker he could not hold a candle to either Amr Bey or Mahmoud Karim. He made his reputation on his astonishing speed. I first saw him playing in the All India Professional Championship when … he was 28 but he did not at that time strike me as being very special.'

Tell that to Jack, who could not imagine anyone having been better than his bald-headed, barrel-chested, giggling friend. As Peter (now Lord) Palumbo said in his magnificent eulogy at Jack's memorial service: 'Jack would put forward the arguments for Hashim's supremacy lucidly and logically, backed up by the sort of analysis and statistics that come from a highly intelligent mind; an extraordinarily shrewd reading of the game; and from assessing the strengths and weaknesses of a particular player in a game of chess.' Asked what his indelible memory was of Hashim, Jack replied, 'The smell of burning rubber from the soles of his shoes'.

Jack and Hashim used to play for a bet, the prize being a pot of tea at a local corner house. The gulf between them, Jack used to say, was such that Hashim could give him an 8-0 start in each game and he could never win enough games to earn himself a free tea.

To celebrate Jack's 50 years as a teaching pro, Peter Palumbo staged a celebration at the Club late in 1985. It began with Jack knocking up gently with Mike Oddy. Jack was unfazed when Oddy left the court, to change his racket, and a small man wearing a wig, a false moustache and dark glasses entered. Jack immediately recognised his old friend Hashim, who had been flown in from Denver, Colorado, for the occasion.

At Pall Mall, Jack made his mark as a teacher, in which role he was sensational. 'I went to Jack almost four years ago unable to play squash although I fooled myself that I could hit a ball around a court,' the late Nigel Dempster, the diarist in the *Daily Mail*, wrote in 1978. 'I shudder to think exactly what Jack must have thought as he took me through a knock-up but clearly he felt that he could be of assistance. Since then the high spot of my week has been my 30 minutes' tuition – part practice, part play and part theory – from someone I regard as the finest teacher in the land. At no time have I felt embarrassed by my ineptitude (a mark of a good pro) and slowly my game has improved to a point where I can actually play squash.'

Jack meant many things to us at the Club. He was of course the squash pro, but he was a friend, a counsellor, a companion. He had enormous dignity and commanded respect. 'He was a lovely, lovely man with whom it was a pleasure to have a conversation and spend time,' Tim Jenkins, a former committee member, said.

Tony Kaye tried to persuade Jack to talk about his experiences when he was a 'tail-end Charlie', a rear gunner in RAF bombers during the Second World War. 'The rear turret on those planes was a cold, lonely and very dangerous place and the rear gunner was the main defence for the bomber since German fighters usually attacked from behind,' Kaye said. 'The eyes of an alert rear gunner were the salvation of many bomber crews. Sometimes they

Jack Giles (right) chats with Brian Phillips (centre) and Chris Campbell. Campbell had been a key member of the team that had brought Giles to Pall Mall in the 1950s, while Phillips was instrumental in having court one renamed in Jack's honour in 1986.

removed the Perspex in order to see better even though that must have made it bitterly cold. Their life expectancy was lower than for other members of a bomber crew. On a tour of 30 sorties their chances of survival were little better than one in four.

'That Jack survived is an incredible tribute to his courage. Can you imagine going on bombing raids night after night knowing that your chances of surviving were so slim? Jack would never give me any personal information. He would never say if he had shot down any other aircraft nor that he had been attacked on any of these missions, though given the figures above he must have been attacked many times. The only thing he did say vis-à-vis fear was that Len Deighton got it absolutely right in his book *Bomber*.'

I had regular lessons from Jack for a dozen years. 'I made my way down to the basement of Pall Mall and found myself on court with a dapper man who seemed to be able to move around without his feet touching the ground,' I wrote in 1987. 'At least I never heard a sound. I also noticed that he concealed his shots with as much guile as a leg spinner.

Sometimes I wouldn't have the faintest idea where the next shot was coming from.'

Whatever time of day it was when you went down to the subterranean changing rooms, you could see Jack's influence. There was the shop with the name 'Jack Giles MBE' on the door. Sit down and get ready for a game and he might ghost past on his way for a quick cigarette or to court one, the Giles Court, named in his honour in 1986. As he passed, you could be sure that someone would shout out 'Hello, Jack. How are you?' because he was a very popular man. And you could be just as sure that he would reply, because he always did, by saying 'Oh, hello' with a note of genuine warmth in his voice, followed by 'I'm very well, thank you. How are you?'

I used to visit him in his basement cubbyhole at lunchtime, where I would usually find him with the remains of his lunch on a tray, his feet up on a chair, a cigarette burning in an ashtray and a copy of *Motor* or *Autocar* in his hands. I still smile when I think of the words we used to say goodbye to one another after our

It was hard, even impossible, to imagine the squash courts at Pall Mall without him

lunchtime chats. 'Bye, Jack. I'll see you next week,' I would say, and he would reply as he always did, 'All being well'.

At first we talked about squash, but as I got to know him better (and he me) our conversation moved to discussions about Hashim and the Khans, about cars, about life in general. I even learned about after-dinner speaking from listening to him at the annual squash dinner. In a riotous, noisy evening when jokes were not all that flew around the room, the only moments when complete silence was guaranteed were when Jack was on his feet talking modestly and drily.

In 1985 Jack reached the retirement age of 65. By then he had been at the Club for almost 30 years and apart from holidays and occasional sickness had given six lessons each day for five days for 45 weeks each year, 40,000 or more. It was hard, even impossible, to imagine the squash courts at Pall Mall without him, and he kindly agreed to stay on for up to five years. Less than two years later, however, on the night of the Club finals and the ensuing squash dinner, he indicated he had had enough. 'I've handed in my resignation,' he said quietly to me.

Jack hardly had time to enjoy his retirement. In midsummer 1989 he died suddenly of a heart attack after playing (and certainly teaching) a man half his age.

Kevin Lewis

Kevin Lewis succeeded Jack after representatives of the squash committee had sat with management in the Mall Room at Pall Mall and interviewed half a dozen candidates. Kevin was personable, young and it was thought that not only could he become a good teacher but he could also cope with the sort of off-court requirements that Jack had been so good at – the annual dinner, marking Bath Club Cup matches, and the like. He began working at the Club in 1987.

Kevin Lewis, who was our professional for 18 months from the autumn of 1987.

His time as our professional was in marked contrast to that of both Oke and Jack. Whereas his two predecessors had served the needs of the Club's members for three-quarters of a century, Kevin lasted only 18 months in the post. He resigned as our squash professional in April 1989.

Greg Pearman

In 1989 Greg Pearman was coaching at Richmond Town Squash Club on the southwestern edge of London, and making a success of it. He was big, strong and personable and had a winning smile that made him an easy person to like. He was 28 and had been a pro for six years. Thinking it was time for a change, he considered moving to San Francisco, but all that altered when he received a telephone call from Bob Johnson, a long-term friend and former England international, who was in the squash equipment business. 'There's a job going at the Royal Automobile Club,' Johnson said. 'I think you should apply for it.'

Greg got busy on his application. 'I had never been to the Club and although I knew London pretty well I didn't know the part of London where the Club was,' he recalled. He got Jonny Leslie to act as one referee, Sir Michael Edwardes as another –

as powerful a pair of referees as you could want. Edwardes, like Greg, was a member of Richmond Town, and had seen him grow up alongside his daughter, Judy, also a promising player. Edwardes recalls that some of the characteristics Greg has now were evident when he was a teenager. 'Boys of 14 and 15 often make a balls of certain things,' Edwardes said. 'Greg didn't. He was very grown up for his age. He was personable, well behaved and mature.'

Occasionally, Jonny Leslie used to go to Richmond Town on a Saturday morning for a game with the promising juniors there. Greg was one and Jamie Hickox, who would go on to win the Drysdale Cup in 1983, was another. Leslie's practice was to put a £1 coin in the front of a court and play juniors for that coin, giving them a five-point start. 'He was tough,' Greg said, smiling. 'He had no qualms about taking a quid from a 15-year-old.'

'Greg was a very callow youth and a very callow squash player when we first started playing,' Leslie recalled. 'He was easy pickings. He was a bit ungainly. He needed to get all his limbs together. He had a lot of development to make. But it was noticeable how keen he was to play and even then he had a tremendous work ethic. I played him regularly for perhaps seven years and in that time he improved from me giving him a five points start to where the games became hard fought and even.'

Greg Pearman, currently Head of Racquets, who arrived at Pall Mall in 1989 as successor to Kevin Lewis.

Greg may have thought that with two such well-known supporters he had a good chance of being offered the job at the Club. He took his application papers and dropped them off in Pall Mall and forgot about things until he was called for an interview. 'Then I walked into the Club, looked around and fell in love with it,' Greg said. 'My father was an architect and he had told me a bit of the history of the place. I was fascinated by it, by the atmosphere, how quaint it was. Charles Day, who was then sports manager, showed me round. My eyes got wider and wider.'

I, as chairman of the squash committee, and Peter Trimingham, the deputy, did most of the interviewing for this job. 'Greg had an immediate presence,' I recalled later. 'He seemed to have to fold himself up to settle into a chair. But he spoke well. I used to say to prospective pros that we had a very distinct membership, that they had to be prepared to coach courtiers and commoners. Greg nodded at that. He didn't seem to think that was a problem. He was ambitious. He wanted to carry on playing

ABOVE: *The current team of professionals – assistant professionals Mark 'Sparky' Jackson (left) and Lauren Briggs and Head of Racquets Greg Pearman.* FACING PAGE: *'Water leaks in to it from time to time, rackets lean against a wall, pieces of paper with scrawled messages on them lie on a desk. Untidy as it might look, this is the heart of the Pall Mall squash community.' Mark Jackson at work in the professionals' office in the squash area.*

competitive squash in the evenings and at weekends, which was a worry for us. Remember we had just had a bad experience with Kevin Lewis which we did not want to repeat. Kevin was getting injured in matches outside the Club and as a result was often unable to perform as our pro. We didn't want to jump out of the frying pan and into the fire. We had reservations about Greg in that regard.

'Furthermore, some members of the committee thought he was too young to take over such a big job. I remember being warned too that if we paid him as much as he wanted then it would knock the Club's salary structure off balance. Others in the know thought that Greg's temperament and his youth might make it difficult for him to survive in such an atmosphere.'

Greg is a gentleman and if he gives his word then he will honour it

So somewhat reluctantly Greg's application was turned down. Not long after this, he bumped into Sir Michael Edwardes. 'How did you get on with the Royal Automobile Club?' Edwardes asked his lanky friend. 'Not very well,' Greg replied. 'They turned me down. I am too young, apparently. And they were worried about my wanting to carry on playing competitive squash.' Later Greg would recall that Edwardes gave a snort of disapproval and said something like 'I'll see about that'.

Soon after this, I heard that Edwardes had said we were making a big mistake in not taking on Greg. 'Greg is a gentleman and if he gives his word then he will honour it,' Edwardes said. With that the committee reconsidered matters. 'Greg himself offered a constructive solution to the money question by volunteering to lower his retainer, which was paid by the Club, and increase his playing fees,' I wrote. 'This was welcomed. Shortly after that I telephoned a number Greg had given me. I thought it would be his home but later discovered it was a public phone box at Richmond Town Squash Club that Greg used as his office. By chance he was passing the phone box at the precise moment I was ringing it. He answered the phone and was delighted when I offered him the job.'

It is fair to say that from that moment to this, Greg has moved the Pall Mall squash section on in a way that is remarkable. He has not done it single-handedly but he has been the driving force, leading his team of Mark Jackson and Lauren Briggs and, from time to time in the past, other coaches as well. In addition to the lessons he gives at Pall Mall, Greg oversees the squash and tennis professionals at Woodcote Park and spends one day a week there. As a result his official title is now Head of Racquets, the spelling of which harks back to days gone by.

Greg's office is a couple of paces from the courts, a room that is a direct descendant of the pokey cubbyhole Jack Giles had 30 years earlier. Water leaks in to it from time to time, rackets lean against a wall, pieces of paper with scrawled messages on them lie on a desk. Untidy as it might look, this is the heart of the Pall Mall squash community.

'Greg has made a major contribution to the atmosphere and climate of the Club,' Sir Michael Edwardes stated. 'His contribution has gone beyond squash. I think he has been outstanding.' Jonny Leslie, the second of the two members who provided references for Greg all those years ago, added, 'He has galvanised the place. What has impressed me has been how he has enthused so many more people about squash in the Club.'

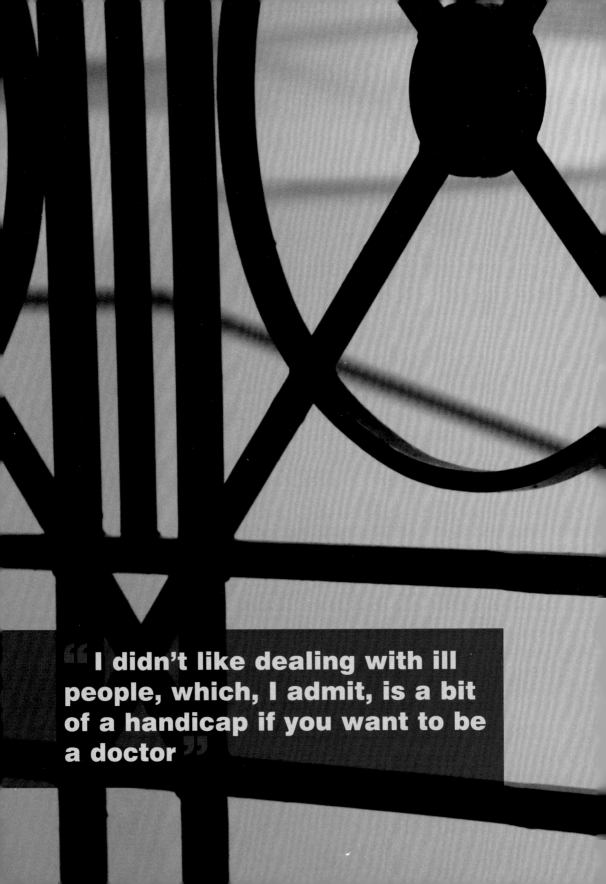

> " I didn't like dealing with ill people, which, I admit, is a bit of a handicap if you want to be a doctor "

Ten of
the Best

Thousands of members have played and watched squash at the Club over the past 100 years. Some have been extraordinary for their achievements at the game and some for their feats in other fields. In celebration of those members who have used our courts since 1911, here are portraits of ten of them.

Amr Bey

Abdel Fattah Amr, who became known as Amr Bey, was the greatest squash player of his generation – and there are those who believe of many other generations as well. He dominated squash in the 1920s and 1930s. Born in Egypt on 14 February 1910, he

came to Britain for the first time in 1928 as a member of his country's Davis Cup team. Rex Bellamy's *The Story of Squash* tells us that Dan Maskell, then a junior pro at Queen's Club, was introduced to Amr Bey who wanted a game of tennis. Unable to find an empty court they moved to a squash court. By the end of this, Amr's first venture on to a squash court, Amr was matching Maskell stroke for stroke.

Being able to make such progress so quickly indicated that Amr Bey was exceptionally gifted. Soon after this game he returned to Egypt to join the diplomatic corps, only to be sent back to London to work in the Egyptian embassy. While in London, Amr Bey

The great Amr Bey, pictured on court in 1934. Besides being the best squash player of his time, Amr Bey was a career diplomat and was Egypt's ambassador to Britain from 1945 to 1952.

joined the Club, where he learned a great deal from Oke Johnson, our professional, a story that is told elsewhere in this book. Within three years Amr Bey was rated the best player in the world. From 1932 he was undefeated in challenges for the British Open and from 1931 won all six of the Amateur Championships in which he competed, losing just 28 points in total in the latter five of his six finals. Amr Bey also won the Club's Open Championship ten years in a row, starting in 1929.

In 1938 Amr Bey announced his retirement from major competitive squash, though he continued to play for the Club in the Bath Club Cup. After the Second World War, Amr Bey returned to Britain, this time as ambassador, and later retired to live in Berkshire.

> **From 1932 he was undefeated in challenges for the British Open and from 1931 won all six of the Amateur Championships in which he competed**

In size Amr Bey resembled Hashim Khan in that he was little more than 5ft 6ins tall. He had Hashim's speed around the court, too, and was nicknamed the 'Human Streak of Lightning'. He was well known for his sportsmanship, and an example of this came after he had once beaten Jim Dear in the British Open, only to discover that Dear had been suffering from a poisoned finger. Anxious to applaud Dear's attitude in playing on uncomplainingly, he asked the secretary of the Club to write a note of appreciation to Dear. Hubert Winterbotham, editor of *Squash Rackets Annual*, wrote of Amr Bey, 'His old world courtesy, his wonderful spirit of sportsmanship and his unfailing kindliness to young players have introduced a lovable note into a game which, at times, is apt to become a little too grim.'

Tennis and Squash magazine summed Amr Bey up rather breathlessly: 'Perhaps we shall live to see a greater artist at the game ... but it seems unlikely. His touch, his speed, his strokes are all perfection and his fame – no matter how long after – will live in the memory like the name of Grace in cricket and of Doherty in lawn tennis. He makes pygmies of us all; he strides over us ... like some fantastic Pan, piping a tune that we try to follow but cannot play.'

Such was the regard in which Amr Bey was held that at the 2009 World Squash

Awards dinner held at the Club he was posthumously honoured with a lifetime achievement award.

Brian Phillips

Brian Phillips was a Club member for over 50 years – a tall, slightly stern-looking man with an engaging conversational manner and a good sense of humour. He is remembered for his services to squash as a player, administrator and unofficial historian.

Born in London in 1916, Phillips won our Open six times and was often said to be the best player never to have won the British Amateur. He was a key player in the Club's pre- and postwar teams that dominated the Bath Club

BELOW AND RIGHT: *Brian Phillips – squash player, squash administrator and squash historian. In 1948/49 he became the first amateur to reach the final of the British Open, losing to Mahmoud Karim of Egypt. Later, Phillips was instigator and custodian of the Pall Mall 'squash museum', and the right-hand photograph, from the December 1988 issue of* Pell-Mell & Woodcote, *shows him modelling a range of memorabilia.*

Cup, a personal highlight coming in the 1950/51 season, when with Phillips playing at second string the Club won every match. He was a member of a Squash Rackets Association team that toured South Africa in 1955, by which time, aged 39, he was past his peak: he had lost his best squash-playing years, from age 23 to 29, to the war. Though he was quite tall, action photographs suggest that he had little difficulty in playing technically correct squash; indeed, he wrote a coaching manual.

Phillips joined the squash committee in October 1946 and was still a member at the time of his death in 1992. With such a span of experience, huge depth of knowledge and a keen mind, he came to be regarded as the unofficial historian on squash matters at the Club. He wrote the authoritative account of how the Drysdale Cup came into being, for example, and another of his articles dealt with the first 50 years of squash at the

Club. Later Phillips was solely responsible for gathering the items that make up the collection of memorabilia in the squash area and on the walls of the squash gallery. It was his idea that courts one and two should be named after Jack Giles and Oke Johnson respectively as a mark of respect.

Less well known is that Phillips was a prisoner of war in Germany in the Second World War. In that understated way the military have of writing about what must have been terrible times, he made it seem that life in *Oflag* VIIB was tolerable. Nevertheless, he and a fellow inmate made a successful escape. They walked for 12 days before linking up with fleeing Russians and then handing themselves over to US forces.

With such a span of experience, huge depth of knowledge and a keen mind, he came to be regarded as the unofficial historian on squash matters at the Club

Phillips's return journey to Britain was circuitous. It involved a pony and trap, being flown via Nuremberg to Paris, three nights in the French capital ('There are worse deaths than three nights in the French capital,' he wrote), then on to Wing aerodrome in Buckinghamshire from which he made his way to London to meet a car that would take him to his home in Kent.

'I made the car pick-up point the [Club],' he wrote, 'and my first port of call was to the squash courts and there in his underground room was Oke Johnson who gave me a tremendous welcome and even persuaded the dressing room attendant to find me clothes to change into for a reunion game of squash. Everything was fixed except shoes so I played Johnnie in socks and slipped all over the place …

'Then it was time to collect my transport and make my way home and meet my parents and someone who had accepted my engagement ring in September 1939 and, lucky me, was still waiting for me in May 1945.'

Phillips died on 12 February 1992. A memorial service at which Norman Borrett, five times Amateur champion, gave an address, was held on 8 April that year.

Sir Nigel Broomfield

If you happened to be around the basement at Pall Mall in the 1950s, you might have heard a series of cracks coming from the general direction of the squash courts during the Drysdale Cup. Gunshot-like, these cracks weren't from the rifle range, which ran behind the courts, but were the sounds of forehand drives by Nigel Broomfield, a prodigy at squash who seemed to be able to generate more power in his strokes than almost anyone at the time or since.

Talent like Broomfield's comes along rarely. A force at rackets and real tennis besides squash, he was also a good enough full-back to have played rugby union for Cambridge University for most of the 1958/59 season, though injury prevented him getting his Blue. He winced slightly at the memory of the match against Cardiff. 'Cardiff's fly-half was a man named Morgan who hoisted high ball after high ball, testing me to the full. There was nothing for it. I had to stand my ground and be hit simultaneously by three men called Bleddyn.'

In January 1958 Broomfield was Amateur champion without losing a game, becoming at 20 the youngest to win this tournament

Broomfield won the Drysdale Cup for the first time at 14, was champion twice more and then did not enter in the final year for which he was eligible because by then he was a squash Blue at Cambridge. He first represented England aged 18, going on to become, according to John Horry in *The History of Squash Rackets*, 'the leader of a golden age of British squash which with J.G.A. Lyon and M.A. Oddy dominated squash in England as well as other parts of the world'. In January 1958 Broomfield was Amateur champion without losing a game, becoming at 20 the youngest to win this tournament as he had earlier been the youngest to win the Drysdale Cup. He took the Amateur again in January 1959, when it was held at Pall Mall, beating Ibrahim Amin in the final for the second year in succession.

'In the nicest possible way Nigel was a bit of a bruiser,' David Jude, who would himself win the Drysdale in 1957, said. 'He cruised around imperiously despatching the ball and his opponents with apparent ease. He was so powerful.' But he was later to

BELOW LEFT: *Like a shot from a gun. Nigel Broomfield's forehand drive resounded around the Pall Mall courts in the 1950s.* BELOW RIGHT: *A 1957 letter to Broomfield from Ian Dear, the squash committee chairman, asking if he would like to play for the Club against Cambridge University, rather than the other way around, so that the talented Broomfield would get a good game.*

develop a slow game, and it was this mastery of both styles of play that helped him win his second Amateur.

Having achieved so much so young, what might Broomfield have gone on to accomplish at squash? We shall never know, for his intelligence and restless mind made him pursue a career in the Army and after that the Foreign Office. For a time he more or less retired from squash. The Club occasionally lured him back to the Pall Mall courts in the 1970s and even the 1980s, by which time he had become a diplomat. Broomfield was ambassador in East Berlin from 1988 to 1990, at the time of the fall of the Berlin Wall, and ambassador to Germany from 1993 to 1997. He was knighted in 1993.

Broomfield's presence at Club matches was always a pleasure because he was an entertaining raconteur and genial companion. Born a left-hander, he was made to do everything right-handed to fit in with the thinking of the time. The exception is in

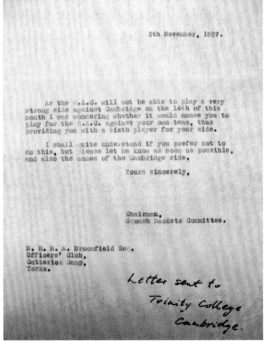

and fell back on the trick of paraphrasing the old adage that "in the land of the blind, the one-eyed man is king". It was a funny old day, both sides had a good time and Tony and Jim got over it – eventually.'

In retirement Markwick lives in London and is an active user of the Club and its facilities.

Nigel Dempster

You always knew when Nigel Dempster was around the squash courts. Either there would be an expletive coming from their direction or he would be in the changing room unwrapping a clean shirt (he was fastidious about his dress) or having a shave on his way in to the office at the *Daily Mail* where he wrote the Diary. Dempster was 'a bigger celebrity than most of the people he writes about,' Peter Tory, a former colleague, put it in 1983. The story was told in his obituary of how 'ex-King Constantine of Greece and King Hussein of Jordan collided at Harry's Bar in London in their eagerness to say hello to him'.

Never a really good squash player, Dempster was nevertheless a regular one who played each week with Jack Giles. He was a great supporter of the Club's facilities and a lively man at the annual squash dinner, particularly when he felt Neale Stainton had made one outburst too many. After his fondness for the Club's Turkish bath had been discovered, Dempster contributed significantly to its redesign and refurbishment. 'The first time I used the bath at the Club was in 1966 and I realised I'd discovered heaven. Your body needs to sweat. That's a rule of life and I see the bath as a way of cleansing myself. There's no better method of clearing one's head, body and pores.'

Born in Calcutta, the only son of an Australian mining engineer whose grandfather had emigrated from Perth in Scotland to Perth in Western Australia in 1829, Dempster came to England at the end of the Second World War and went to Sherborne, which school he was asked to leave when he was 16. 'I didn't mind in the least,' he said. 'I was fed

> **The first time I used the bath at the Club was in 1966 and I realised I'd discovered heaven. Your body needs to sweat**

up with being beaten every three weeks anyway. I held the school record for beatings.'

Dempster's diary in the *Daily Mail* made his name and he joined the Club about the time he started writing it. It is unusual for journalists to associate with the people they write about. Dempster, however, who was married and divorced twice, to a granddaughter of the 11th Marquess of Queensberry and to Lady Camilla, daughter of the 11th Earl of Leeds, did so seemingly without any embarrassment. His strength, according to one obituarist, was considerable knowledge and a good memory. 'At a party he would know who used to be married to whom, how they made their money, what schools they went to and – most importantly – who they were sleeping with.'

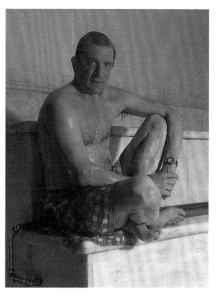

Nigel Dempster enjoyed Pall Mall's Turkish bath and the Daily Mail *diarist was involved in its refurbishment.*

Dempster once explained how he brought off this rather difficult trick of being a poacher while associating with the gamekeepers. 'At times like these I have to dissociate myself from Nigel Dempster gossip columnist and assume the role of Nigel Dempster [Royal Automobile Club] member. It's the same with the Royal Family. Sometimes I've written less than flatteringly about one of them and Prince Michael is president of the Club. At some clubs I would have been drummed out long ago. I was not and I think that shows maturity and what a good club it is. The worst I can do is spoil someone's Weetabix the following morning.'

Dempster died on 12 July 2007 from the effects of progressive supranuclear palsy, a rare brain condition.

Stuart Courtney

Little did Stuart Courtney realise when he walked into Pall Mall one evening in 1966 how much his future life was going to be linked with squash in general and the Club in particular. On that night more than 40 years ago, Courtney, then 16, was playing Chris Orriss, 18, in the final of the Drysdale Cup, in a meeting of left-handers, of men who

The Squash Gallery

More faces from the Pall Mall squash section.

THIS PAGE: *1 Simon Lambert;
2 Neil Watts and James Maskey, 2010;
3 Chris Burrows, 2005; 4 Neil Cottle and
Steve Pearce, 2009; 5 David Garrett, 2010;
6 Barrie Brien and Andrew Wakely, 2010;
7 Marco Sodi, 2009; 8 James Meyer, 2007.*

THIS PAGE: 1 Charles Fuente and James Dubois, 2004; 2 David Harper, 2005;
3 Graham Nichols, 2005; 4 David Rawle; 5 Geoff Gelardi, 2007;
6 Mark Jackson, 2007; 7 Richard Ford, 2007; 8 Arnie Isaacson and
Hugh Moxon, 2004.

would go on and become two of the Club's leading lights. Orriss won the first two games narrowly, lost the next two comfortably and

Stuart Courtney, flanked by Jonny Leslie (left) and Philip Kenyon, at the Squash Rackets Association's Golden Jubilee dinner at Pall Mall in December 1978.

won the fifth and the trophy despite scoring fewer points than Courtney overall. 'The press wrote "the younger man was clearly the better player",' Orriss said wryly.

Indeed, Courtney's shot-making helped him win the Drysdale for the next two years running and took him quickly on to become one of Britain's most accomplished players. In an international career that started in 1971/72 and ended in 1980/81, he won 12 caps for England and 14 for Great Britain, whom he represented in two World Amateur Championships, the second at Birmingham in 1976, which Britain won. He was also, of course, a Bath Club Cup player for the Club. Meanwhile, his wife Jane was British women's number one.

A gifted sportsman who played schoolboy cricket for Surrey and Middlesex, was twice amateur champion at Eton fives and was above average at tennis as well,

Courtney played squash that was a dazzling confection of the brilliant, the eye-opening, the wildly ambitious and the occasionally workmanlike. Others powered their way around courts and past their opponents; Courtney was graceful and quick-footed, one who could bring off some sensationally daring shots and always tried to do so.

Having grown up playing on the cold courts at Dulwich Squash Club, Courtney took time to get accustomed to the temperature and pace of our courts. 'I found the heat of the courts difficult and lost to people I did not expect to lose to,' he said. 'But once I achieved a decent level of fitness it was never a problem again. I made it work for me. I came to love playing on number one court. I won more there than I lost. I preferred it to playing on the Bruce Court. It was lighter, more airy, took a shot better. It seemed wider. The Bruce Court was popular because of the viewing facilities.'

Courtney has won a wider range of squash competitions at Pall Mall than anyone: the Open in 1980, 1983, 1984 and 1987; the Lowenthal Veterans Trophy in 1998, 1999, 2002, 2003 and 2004; and the Herbert Vintage Squash Rackets Cup in 2005. He and Malcolm Lees won the Edwardes–Berman Doubles Trophy in 2000 and 2004.

For a number of years he worked for the family contract cleaning and maintenance firm started by his grandfather in 1904. Later Courtney became chief executive of what was then the Squash Rackets Association but which soon became England Squash & Racketball.

Courtney left the governing body in 2001 and now works in the building services business. He has retired completely from squash.

James Hunt

No other motor racing world champion has played squash for the Royal Automobile Club. James Hunt joined the Club in 1970, when he was 23, and wanted to play Bath Club Cup squash. In those days I used to manage the team in that competition and I found him to be a useful man to have available, even if he did sometimes tax my patience.

'Often I would be in the changing room fretting until I heard the clip, clip, clip of his shoes as he came down the staircase,' I wrote in *Pell-Mell & Woodcote* in June 1993 just after his death. The next moment he would burst in full of apologies. 'Some silly sod tried to carve me up going round Clapham Common,' he would say. 'I had to sort

BELOW: *'No other motor racing world champion has played squash for the Royal Automobile Club.' James Hunt – Formula 1 champion in 1976 and a Bath Club Cup winner with the Club's first team in 1984.* FACING PAGE: *Michael Edwardes (left) is probably still best remembered outside the Club for his work with British Leyland. Within it, though, Edwardes is known as a doubles enthusiast, and is pictured here with his squash partner, fellow South African Toddy Berman.*

him out. I took him on the inside on the next bend. He didn't know whether he was coming or going. Serve him right.' Manoeuvres like this were not the reason he had the nickname 'Hunt the Shunt' in his early days as a motor racing driver, but they might have been. His tardy arrival would sometimes be forgiven by his bringing a spectacular girlfriend with him.

Hunt was Formula 1 world champion in 1976, but it is not for us to assess his

driving ability. That is best left to others. As a squash player he had many attributes. One of his contemporaries remembers Hunt as 'bustling around the court, slightly round shouldered. He was not naturally gifted but he was fit, aggressive and very determined.' In that *Pell Mell & Woodcote* article, I wrote, 'His technique was individual, based on fast darting steps around the court accompanied by the odd

expletive. With his hair flying he chased every shot, ricocheting off the side walls, gasping for breath, living his squash to the full as he did his life. He was not stylish but that did not matter because he never knew when he was beaten. An added bonus was that over dinner he would recount tales of fast cars and beautiful women. Or was it the other way round?'

In later years Hunt used to cycle to the Club from Wimbledon, where he lived with his children and his collection of canaries, budgerigars and parrots. He would discard his shorts and change into a shirt and jacket on the pavement outside Pall Mall before heading down to the courts. He was a regular in our first team in the Bath Club Cup in 1984, the year we won both the first and second divisions of the competition – a notable achievement even for a club as steeped in squash as we are. A photograph of the two teams hangs in the squash gallery.

Despite the image he had of being a playboy, Hunt only occasionally stayed to enjoy the socialising after a match, though he did attend the Club for the 70th anniversary celebration of the Bath Club Cup competition in May 1993. He arrived late, was jolly and friendly but departed early. 'The last sight many of us would have had of him was of his leaving the Mountbatten Room waving farewell with his hand in the air without so much as turning his head,' I wrote. '"Bye James," someone shouted out.' It was prophetic. We did not see him alive again. Hunt died on 15 June 1993, aged 45.

Sir Michael Edwardes

Known in the Club for his enthusiasm for doubles squash and the considerable part he has played in the expansion of that form of the game, Michael Edwardes, who was 80 in October 2010, will forever be associated in the wider world with his tribulations at British Leyland, the strike-torn car manufacturer, in the late 1970s and early 1980s. Various businessmen had tried to solve the difficulties faced by British Leyland, and failed. But where others may have hesitated when offered the top job at the company in 1977, Edwardes did not. 'If one is asked to take on a difficult challenge it isn't a question of saying "Shall I say yes?"' he reasoned. 'It is a question of saying "Can I say no?"'

For some years Edwardes was constantly in the news as he wrestled with the problems at one of Britain's biggest manufacturing concerns. 'He's a marathon man, answering your questions in a steady, economical way with a measured pace, neither hurrying to the heart of the matter nor dawdling over detail,' Nick Valery, motor industry correspondent of *The Economist*, wrote in 1979. That applies just as much 30 years later. He remains quietly spoken and authoritative. 'Michael has the knack of saying things that make you stop and think to yourself, "Why didn't I think of that?"' Peter Trimingham, a friend and fellow doubles player, said.

Having brought British Leyland back from the brink, Edwardes found he had more time at

his disposal and reacquainted himself with a game he had played at school and at Rhodes University in Grahamstown, South Africa. 'I gave my golf clubs to a pretty girl and returned to squash,' he said. During his term as president of the Squash Rackets Association he did all he could to further the cause of modern doubles. He is credited with getting doubles squash started at Woodcote Park, which certainly helped in the campaign to have a doubles court built at Pall Mall. 'But it's not right to give me all the credit,' Edwardes said. 'Brian [McGivern, then chairman of the Pall Mall and Woodcote Park boards] made it happen. He has not sought the credit but he deserves it.'

I gave my golf clubs to a pretty girl and returned to squash

Ever since his return to squash, the doubles game has been an important part of Edwardes's life, whether at Pall Mall or Woodcote Park, or at St Francis Bay near Port Elizabeth in South Africa, where he has a holiday home. At the St Francis Bay Squash Club there are two glass-backed doubles courts, one named the Michael Edwardes Court. A doubles tournament takes place there each spring, and 64 pairs competed in it in 2010. Though suffering from Parkinson's disease, Edwardes moves through life at a cracking pace, still putting in a day's work at his office in Weybridge and playing squash regularly at Pall Mall and Woodcote Park.

Peter Chalk

Every club has its characters. One of ours is Peter Chalk, a Peter Pan figure with a mischievous smile and an ability to see the funny side of most situations. 'Chalky' is in his mid-seventies, looks 20 years younger and occasionally behaves as if he is still in his twenties. National service put paid to his plans to study law at Cambridge, so he got his physics, chemistry and biology O levels in one year in order to do medicine at Barts. 'I was soon thrown out of there because I didn't do any work and I drank too much,' he said. 'Plus, I didn't like dealing with ill people, which, I admit, is a bit of a handicap if you want to be a doctor.'

Chalk became articled to a firm of chartered accountants in London who paid him £4 2s 6d (£4 13p) each month. At the same time he devoted himself seriously to squash, playing Azam Khan at the New Grampians club every week and also taking part in competitions at the Grafton club in south London. He had considerable talent and in time beat everyone in England at least once except Jonah Barrington, becoming ranked as high as fifth in Britain. He could also play golf, getting down to 2 handicap and playing in the English Open Amateur Stroke Play championship.

Once retired from competitive squash, Chalk turned his attentions to administration. He was a shrewd if unconventional Great Britain team manager at four world championships from 1971 to 1977. 'When Britain faced Pakistan in a match early in the 1971 world championships in New Zealand, I sent Ayton and Easter to bed to get some sleep and I told Corby that he didn't need to go to bed because he would never beat Aftab Jawaid anyway,' said Chalk. 'Jawaid had won the Amateur three times and been runner-up in the Open twice.'

'An ability to see the funny side of most situations.' Peter Chalk addresses the diners at the Bath Club Cup 85th Anniversary celebration at Pall Mall in 2006.

This apparent put-down so incensed Corby that he took himself off to his room immediately, and the next day, still angry with his team captain, defeated Jawaid. 'When he won, Corby stuck two fingers up at me in the gallery and said, well, you can probably guess what he said,' Chalk added, grinning. 'I shouted back, "Yes, but I'm a very good manager."'

When filling the same role with Britain in the team event at the 1973 World Amateur Championship in South Africa, Chalk demonstrated some ingenuity in thinking up a financial incentive for his players. He bet them – the joint favourites with Australia – that they would not win, giving them odds of 200-1 and suggesting each of them should put down £1. Stuart Courtney's match against Frank Donnelly was thought to be the one that would determine the outcome. When Courtney led 2-1 and 8-5 it looked good for Britain.

'Then, with his opponent lying on the floor at the back of the court gasping for

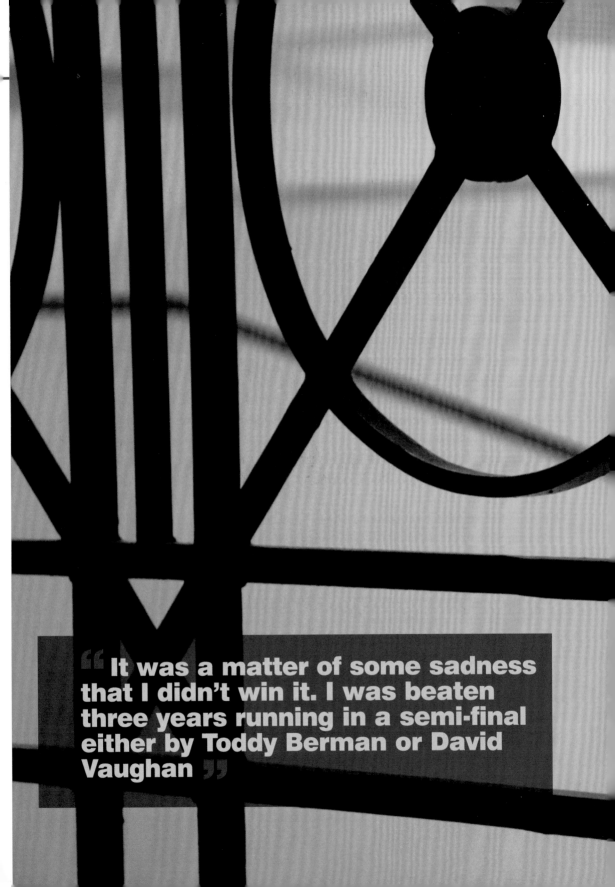

"It was a matter of some sadness that I didn't win it. I was beaten three years running in a semi-final either by Toddy Berman or David Vaughan"

The Trophy Cabinet

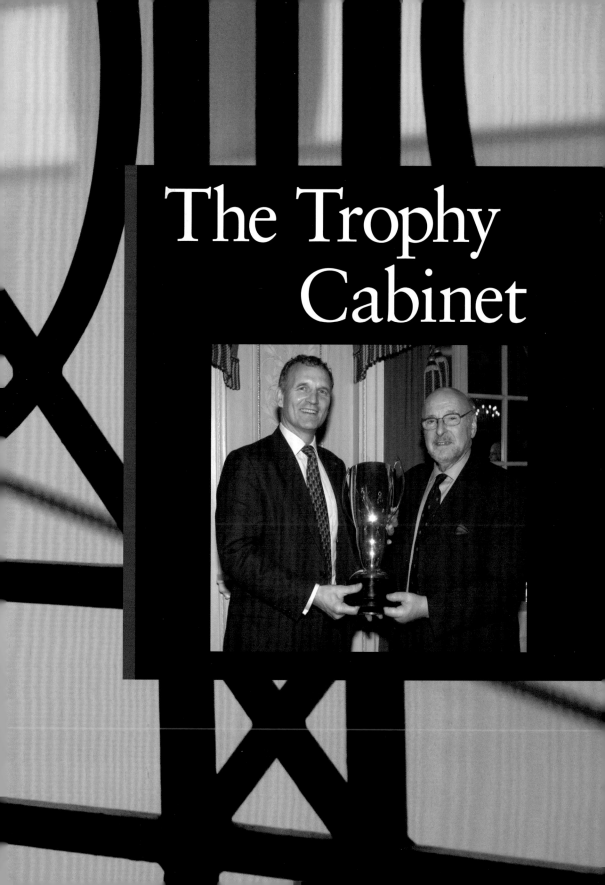

O f the numerous trophy cases around the Pall Mall clubhouse, there are perhaps three that are of special interest to squash players. One of these stands inside the reception area of the squash courts, outside Greg and Mark's office. Almost everyone reading this book will have passed it at one time or another and many of you will have stopped and looked at its contents. It holds some of the memorabilia that members have donated down the years and was lovingly put together in the mid-1980s by Brian Phillips, who had been rightly regarded as something of an authority on squash since his playing days. He donated some of the material himself from his own collection, and dragooned others into contributing objects which he said would be well looked after and well presented. Both promises remain true to this day. Then he used to turn up at squash committee meetings with his latest acquisitions and talk enthusiastically about the Club's 'memorablia' (*sic*).

Among the items in this cabinet are:

- A trophy commemorating Jack Giles's victories in the Professional Championship of the United Kingdom, described as being on loan to the Club from J.H. Giles and donated after his death in 1989 by his widow, Hilda.
- The Evans Cup, a Public Schools under 18 competition, won four times by Nigel Broomfield, and once each by Stuart Courtney and Chris Orriss, among others.
- Brian Phillips's racket used in the final of the 1948/49 British Open – he was the first amateur to reach the final.
- A tankard, presented jointly by Brian and David Phillips when Peter Phillips,

David's father, won the Club's Open Championship in 1956. The significance is that the final was a match between two unrelated men bearing the same surname.

- An example of the Atlas 'Special' racket, donated by the Club.
- The 1936/37 annual of the Squash Rackets Association.
- A six-inch-high silver statue of Amr Bey, lent by R.M.D. Cardew prior to his death.
- The trophy that was competed for in the Amateur Championship before the game went open in 1980. It cost about £20 when contributed by the Club in 1923.

Missing from this cabinet are the trophies the Club members play for in the Open, the Handicap competitions and so on. Also missing are the Drysdale Cup, the Bath Club Cup trophies for the three divisions, and the Londonderry Cup with its remarkable number of plinths. The five last-mentioned trophies – as well as the Open trophy, the B Handicap trophy and the Doubles Handicap trophy, which do not have a named donor – are displayed in the two cabinets in the Rotunda. They are well worth a look.

The Drysdale Cup

The most magnificent-looking trophy of them all, in my eyes, is the Drysdale Cup, awarded each year to the winner of the premier boys' annual event in the world – the under 19 competition at the British

ABOVE: *James Sandwith (right), the squash committee chairman, presents the Doubles Handicap trophy to Grant Macpherson (left) and Nick McMahon at finals night 2009.* FACING PAGE: *A detail of the Club squash honours boards located in the basement at Pall Mall.*

Junior Open Championships. A four-sided trophy well over a foot high, the Drysdale Cup is much bigger and much heavier, for example, than the claret jug given in golf to winners of the Open, the oldest professional major championship in the game.

The story of how the Drysdale Cup came into being and of the competition for which it is presented is interesting and centres on, obviously enough, Dr Theodore

LEFT: *Dr Theodore Drysdale, a squash international and the first secretary of the Squash Rackets Representative Committee, forerunner of the SRA.*
FACING PAGE: *The completed draw for the first Drysdale Cup competition in 1926, won by C.J. Wilson of Repton.*

Drysdale. Drysdale was an all-rounder: a medical doctor who was a good enough squash player to have won the Club's first Open, held in the 1919/20 season, and to have been a member of the Club's three-man Bath Club Cup team that won the first competition in the 1922/23 season. Drysdale also won the Club's Open on two further occasions, in 1920/21 and 1922/23, and was the first honorary secretary of the Tennis & Rackets Association's Squash Rackets Representative Committee, which met for the first time in 1923.

A contemporary described Drysdale as a 'dedicated rather than an instinctive exponent with a racket'. According to Col Alec Kearsey, who knew him well, 'He had phenomenal stamina and was one of the most persevering players that ever competed in the Amateur Championship.' Indeed, Drysdale was one of the country's leading amateurs and won a place in the international team that toured the United States and Canada in 1924.

Yet it is for his cup that Drysdale is better remembered. He had a bee in his bonnet about juniors. He encouraged them and wanted them to have their own championship, for which he was even prepared to donate a trophy. In 1925 he was invited to chair a sub-committee to look into the matter. All was going well until the autumn of that year when Drysdale suffered a mosquito bite which became infected. He was rushed to a nursing home but died of acute septicaemia within a fortnight.

Drysdale's idea of a junior championship was not lost, however. As a personal memorial to a highly regarded colleague, grateful friends at the Club decided to pursue the doctor's vision. A subscription, limited to 5s (25p) per member, realised a fine silver trophy of unique four-faceted

He had a bee in his bonnet about juniors. He encouraged them and wanted them to have their own championship

Junior Amateur Squash Racquets Championship
(THE "DRYSDALE" CUP)
AT THE
ROYAL AUTOMOBILE CLUB,
April 19th—23rd, 1926.

Monday, April 19th	Tuesday, April 20th	Wednesday, April 21	Thursday, April 22nd.	Friday, April 23rd
	G. A. Birch SCRATCHED 11.0 a.m.	Carr. W.O		
G. R. L. Gaunt 11.0 a.m.	Carr 15.8. 15.9.			
H. L. Carr		11.0 a.m.	Carr. 17.14 15.11.	
R. B. C. Ryall 11.0 a.m.	Ryall 15.11. 15.3			
A. B. Marshall		Ryall 15.10. 15.8.		
J. H. B. D. Oldman 11.30 a.m.	Rigden .W.O.			
N. F Rigden			11.0 a.m.	Wilson 15.4 15.4
L. D. Cambridge 11.30 a.m.	Cambridge 15.8. 15.11.			
G. M. Knight		Cambridge 15.11. 15.3		
D. R. Fussell 12.0 Noon	Fussell 8.15. 15.12. 15.7.			
E. M. Buzzard		11.30 a.m.	Wilson 15.4. 15.4	
J. L. Rees 12.0 Noon	Rees W.O.			
E. D. Garnett		Wilson 15.1. 15.3.		
C. J. Wilson 12.30 p.m.	Wilson W.O.			Wilson 15.5 15
A. Kay			11.30 a.m.	
B. G. Wennink 12.30 p.m.	Wennink 6.15. 17.5. 15.9			
F. R. Rea		Fordham 15.2 15.2.		
T. V. N. Anderson 2.30 p.m.	Fordham 17.14			
A. S. Fordham		12.0 Noon	Fordham 4.15. 15.10. 15.17.	
H. Drysdale 2.30 p.m.	Drysdale 15.13 8.10			
R. G. Shaw		Drysdale 15.4. 4.15. 15.11.		
W. C. Carr 3.0 p.m.	Delgado 15.6. 9.16. 15.10.			
G. A. Delgado			11.45 a.m.	Fordham. 15.8. 15.7.
M. O. Long 3.0 p.m.	Ridgers 17.18. 15.4. 15.4			
J. S. Ridgers		Tufnell 15.4. 15.4.		
H. A. Lenox 3.30 p.m.	Tufnell 15.7. 15.17.			
L. Tufnell		12.30 p.m.	Tufnell 15.2. 15.12	
M. K. Garnett 3.30 p.m.	Garnett 15.4. 15.7. 15.2			
A. M. Shepley-Smith		Garnett. W.O.		
	12.30 p.m. A. K. Du Bell			

The Best of Three Games to be played.
Any Competitor failing to put in an appearance within 10 minutes of the booked time will be scratched.
On presentation of this Programme to the Hall Porter (1) Competitors will be allowed to book a Court for practice during the week prior to the Competition and (2) Unsuccessful Competitors will be admitted to view subsequent matches.

8th April, 1926.   **F. P. ARMSTRONG,** *Secretary.*

C.M. Butler of Lancing College, winner of the Drysdale Cup competition in 1936, pictured with the trophy and his replica to keep.

design. A considerable sum must have been raised if we compare the size and value of this trophy with the Bath Club Cup, which cost 50 guineas (£52 50p) in 1922. Named the Drysdale Cup, the new prize was to be competed for by boys aged under 19 on 31 December the previous year. The inaugural competition took place at Pall Mall in April 1926 when it was won by C.J. Wilson of Repton.

From 1926 to 1978 the Club hosted the Drysdale Cup competition, which was administered by members of the Club's squash committee under the watchful eye initially of Oke Johnson and then of Jack Giles, the Club's first two professionals. There was a decided spin-off for the Club in that usually the winner was offered membership without having to pay the one-off joining fee and this led to a number of good players becoming members.

The exact name of the championship for which the trophy is the prize has endured a number of modifications down the years. Held in the second half of the season, the competition was known on the first entry form as the Junior Amateur Squash Racquets Championship for The 'Drysdale' Cup. Underneath these words ran the following: '(Presented by Members of the Royal Automobile Club in Memory of the late Dr. T. Drysdale)'. The word 'Championship' was later deleted at the request of the SRA, and the tournament became known as The Junior Amateur Squash Rackets Competition for the Drysdale Cup. Now part of the British Junior Open Championships, the competition is known as the British Under-19 Open Junior Championship. It is held each January and organised by England Squash & Racketball.

Look at the names engraved on the Drysdale Cup and its plinth. They are a

Look at the names engraved on the Drysdale Cup and its plinth. They are a who's who of squash

who's who of squash. In fact, at the time of writing late in 2010, five of the top six players in the world rankings had won the Drysdale and the sixth was a losing finalist. Looking back, Nigel Broomfield won in 1952 when he was 14 and again in 1954 and 1955; though eligible, he did not enter in 1956. Jeremy Lyon, who played regularly at the Club but never became a member, beat Broomfield to win in 1953. Mike Oddy, soon to become a stalwart of the Club, was champion in 1956. Mike Corby won in 1959 and duly became a powerful presence among squash players at the Club. One year later it was the turn of David Brazier, who became a member for a short time but then resigned when, despite being ranked fourth in Great Britain, he was not selected for the Club's Bath Club Cup team.

In 1966 Chris Orriss, at that time a student at King's College, a part of London University, defeated Stuart Courtney in the final and remembers having the trophy in his room at university without any fear that it might be stolen or damaged. The Club's policy changed later, so that though the recipient was presented with the cup upon winning it, he had to hand it back to the Club immediately afterwards for safe keeping. Having joined the Club late in 1970, Orriss became a member of the squash committee in November 1974 and remains one to this day. Courtney won the Drysdale Cup in 1967 and 1968.

Only one player has won the event four times: Del Harris, who was successful in 1985 and repeated his victory in each of the next three years. M. El Shorbagy of Egypt was champion in 2008, 2009 and 2010. Late in 2010, El Shorbagy was ranked twelfth in the world.

The Open Trophy
Like so many of our trophies, the prize for the winner of the Club's Open is handsome and sizeable. The current trophy is the second to have been played for in this, our premier competition, the first having been presented to Amr Bey for him to keep in 1931 after he had won the

Jonny Leslie, six times winner of the Club's Open, with the trophy.

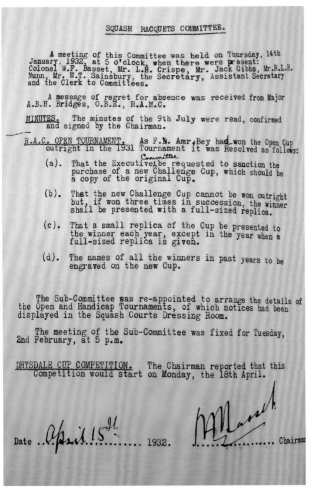

SQUASH RACQUETS COMMITTEE.

A meeting of this Committee was held on Thursday, 14th January, 1932, at 5 o'clock, when there were present: Colonel W.F. Basset, Mr. L.H. Crispe, Mr. Jack Gibbs, Mr.R.L.H. Nunn, Mr. W.T. Sainsbury, the Secretary, Assistant Secretary and the Clerk to Committees.

A message of regret for absence was received from Major A.B.H. Bridges, O.B.E., R.A.M.C.

MINUTES. The minutes of the 9th July were read, confirmed and signed by the Chairman.

R.A.C. OPEN TOURNAMENT. As F.N. Amr Bey had won the Open Cup outright in the 1931 Tournament it was Resolved as follows:

(a). That the Executive Committee be requested to sanction the purchase of a new Challenge Cup, which should be a copy of the original Cup.

(b). That the new Challenge Cup cannot be won outright but, if won three times in succession, the winner shall be presented with a full-sized replica.

(c). That a small replica of the Cup be presented to the winner each year, except in the year when a full-sized replica is given.

(d). The names of all the winners in past years to be engraved on the new Cup.

The Sub-Committee was re-appointed to arrange the details of the Open and Handicap Tournaments, of which notices had been displayed in the Squash Courts Dressing Room.

The meeting of the Sub-Committee was fixed for Tuesday, 2nd February, at 5 p.m.

DRYSDALE CUP COMPETITION. The Chairman reported that this Competition would start on Monday, the 18th April.

Date ...April 15th... 1932. .... Chairman

The squash committee minutes of 14 January 1932, outlining plans for a new Open trophy now that Amr Bey was entitled to keep the original, having won it three times in succession, 1929–31.

Open three times in succession. The Club subsequently supplied a new trophy and made two provisions: that the names of all previous winners be engraved on it and that it be played for in perpetuity. With hindsight the latter stipulation proved wise because Amr Bey won the competition seven more times in a row and could therefore have been entitled to keep two more trophies.

The Wilding Cup

In common with the other named trophies described below, the Wilding Cup is displayed in the Rotunda. Presented annually to the winner of the A Handicap tournament, it is another Club trophy with an interesting history. Its donor, H.F.H. (Henry) Wilding, was a member of the Club from the 1920s. How good a squash player he was is not known, but he was certainly enthusiastic. Starting in April 1930, Wilding began playing regularly against Captain H.E. Harker,

perhaps twice each week because by 1934 they had played 500 games against one another and the score stood exactly all square. We know about it from a newspaper cutting attached to a postcard bearing the address of the Bath Club, mentioning this feat. 'Captain H.E. Harker and H.F.H. Wilding began to play one another on April 7, 1930,' the cutting went. 'On June 20, 1932, Harker led by 161 games to 139. Wilding drew level on February 19 last. And this "squash" marathon is going on!'

SQUASH MARATHON

All square at the end of 500 squash rackets games is the remarkable position in which two members of the R.A.C. find themselves to-day.

Captain H. E. Harker and H. F. H. Wilding began to play one another on April 7, 1930. On June 20, 1932, Harker led by 161 games to 139. Wilding drew level on February 19 last.

And this "squash" marathon is going on!

LEFT: *The press cutting telling of the Harker–Wilding 'squash marathon'.* BELOW: *The photograph of Oke Johnson (left) and Henry Wilding at Pall Mall alluded to by Wilding's son John in his 1978 letter to the Squash Rackets Association.*

We do not know how long this duel continued, but we can assume that Wilding liked regular matches against the same opponent, as his son, John Wilding, shed some light on the matter. 'Father was a very keen player who played for a long time,' John Wilding said. In a letter to the secretary of the Squash Rackets Association dated 11 July 1978, he pointed out that there was a photograph, taken on a Pall Mall court in 1951, of his father standing with Oke Johnson. 'At the time this picture was taken my Father was 75 years of age,' Wilding junior noted. 'He played regularly twice a week with Mr Johnson who was of course the Club's pro at that period.

'I think the picture was taken to mark my Father's forty years of playing squash together with the fact that he was the oldest playing member in the Club. I am not sure how many years the two men played together but I know that my Father never played with anyone else during the later period as this was a promise he made to my Mother, in other words the controlled non competitive game. Nevertheless he always came off court "dripping" and was not satisfied unless this was the case. He continued to play for several more years until he had a fall on court and decided to give up. He lived into his 80th year.'

So here we have, in Henry Wilding, a man who played a lot of squash at the Club for a very long time. 'Father was a very keen player as is obvious from the foregoing,' John Wilding stated. 'And one day when he noticed there was no trophy for the older players he offered to donate

one valued at up to 100 guineas. He envisaged it would be for veterans, players over 50, but said he would leave it to the Committee to decide what competition it would be used for.'

At this time, the mid-1940s, it so happened that the A Handicap competition did not have a trophy. In 1939, the last time it was contested before the Second

The trophy that Turner had lost was found and so the committee decided to make that the prize for the B Handicap

World War, the competition had been won by J.H. Turner. When the Club's squash tournaments started up again after the war, Turner was, according to the minutes of the time, 'unable to inform the Committee of the whereabouts of the cup itself'. The committee therefore decided to use Henry Wilding's gift as the A Handicap trophy and it bears the names of the winners from 1946/47 onwards.

Meanwhile, the B Handicap competition was without a trophy. Like the A Handicap contest, it had first taken place in 1919/20, and the minutes of the squash committee from that time tell us that prize money was given to its winner. However, some time between March and May 1947, the trophy that Turner had lost was

Minutes of the Club's squash committee meeting of 6 March 1947, discussing the Wilding Cup. They note that Mr J.H. Turner was 'unable to inform the Committee of the whereabouts of the [Handicap] cup itself' and imply that Henry Wilding's trophy would take its place.

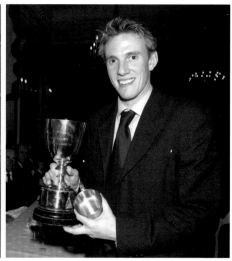

ABOVE LEFT: *Former England number one badminton player Anders Nielsen (left), who died in 2010, is presented with the Wilding Cup for 2007 by James Sandwith.* ABOVE RIGHT: *Hugh Moxon with the B Handicap trophy, having won the 2004 competition. The trophy is the old Handicap Challenge Cup, lost during the Second World War but later rediscovered and assigned to the B Handicap.*

found and so the committee decided to make that the prize for the B Handicap. The names of the winners of the original handicap event, now known as the A Handicap, were left in place and below the last name a new heading, 'Class B', was engraved. From 1947/48 on, the names of the winners refer to the B Handicap competition, while the title on the trophy itself remains the Handicap Challenge Cup.

A family footnote: John Wilding, who is still a member of the Club though he has long since stopped playing squash, clearly inherited something of his father's longevity as a squash player and his propensity for regular games against the same opponent. In a footnote to his 1978 letter to the SRA, he wrote: 'I also play and am a member of the [Royal Automobile Club], Chichester and the mid-Sussex at Horsham, and although in the "vintage" age group still have quite a long way to go before equalling my Father's record.' John Wilding's regular opponent was Harry Lack and they played one another for many years at the Georgian Squash Club in Haslemere.

Lowenthal Veterans Trophy

The Lowenthal Veterans Trophy, played for by competitors aged 45 and over, was presented in 1975 by Laurie Lowenthal, who joined the Club in 1947 and thereafter

Laurie Lowenthal (right), donor of the Lowenthal Veterans Trophy, presents the cup to the 2005 winner, Paul Bourdon, a former British junior tennis champion.

played twice weekly with Jack Giles for 25 years. 'When I got to 45 there was no competition for those of us of that age,' Lowenthal said. 'We could not keep up with the younger ones and we still thought we were too good for those who were older than we were. I dare say I considered giving the game up but I am glad I didn't. If there had been doubles then I would certainly have thought about playing that form of squash but there wasn't.

'I thought it would be a nice thing to do to present a trophy for the over 45s. So I went to Hatton Garden, paid probably somewhere between £50 and £100 for a trophy, had it engraved and presented it to the Club. It was a matter of some sadness that I didn't win it. I was beaten three years running in a semi-final either by Toddy Berman or David Vaughan.'

Herbert Vintage Squash Rackets Cup

The Herbert Vintage Squash Rackets Cup is for singles play by members over 55 and its donor was a man of above average height, a very quiet manner and a dry sense of humour who, like so many, played almost all his squash with Jack Giles. If you were around the changing room when he and Jack were

Andrew Lowenthal (left) takes charge of the Herbert Vintage Squash Rackets Cup for 2010. Lowenthal's father, Laurie, presented the veterans trophy for over 45s, but neither he nor Andrew ever won it.

talking, you would sometimes hear Jack explode in mock indignation – 'MISTER Herbert!' he would say.

G.P. Herbert had the appearance of a lawyer as he always wore a pin-striped suit and waistcoat which rather gave the impression he was on his way to or from the Law Courts. Laurie Lowenthal believes he was a farmer. A slightly mysterious figure, Herbert said very little, paced around the changing room anxiously both before and after games, smoked a lot and was only seen in the squash area during the day.

Stainton Over 65s Cup

First played for in 1994/95, the Stainton Over 65s Cup was presented by Neale Stainton, a much-loved figure around the squash courts, who felt there was a need for a competition for older members. Stainton may be remembered by some for a lively episode involving Nigel Dempster and some butter at a finals night dinner. When Stainton retired from the squash committee a year or two after this incident, he was thanked at the annual dinner and, on behalf of the committee, Dempster presented him with a commemorative silver butter dish.

Stainton was the son of the Chapter Clerk of St George's Chapel, Windsor. He became a solicitor and then chief solicitor in the Post Office Solicitor's department in London. He used to be at the Club almost every day when he was working, often playing squash with Jack Giles. He was a creature of habit, always sitting in the same place in the changing room and nearly always wearing grey flannels and a blazer with a woollen cardigan beneath.

David Mawson received the Stainton Over 65s Cup (pictured over the page) for 2006 and has won the competition every year since, including 2010.

Long after he had retired, up to within five years of his death, Stainton continued to play most weekday mornings with Greg Pearman. Greg once asked him why he carried on playing. 'It's no good letting up,' came the answer. 'I'm not going to die like my friend.' 'Who was that and where did he die?' asked Greg. 'He died right there,' Stainton replied, pointing to a place in the changing room.

Stainton was a good swimmer and was said to have an enlarged heart as a result of all the swimming he did. Soon after he joined the Club, he was swimming in the pool when he found himself being overtaken. This did not happen very often and Stainton was slightly put out. He speeded up but the swimmer next to him still pulled away. When he stopped, Stainton shouted to him, 'I say. You're a very good swimmer. Who are you?' 'Johnny Weismuller' was the reply.

Stainton died on 11 November 2008 and was cremated wearing his Club tie. Maureen, his second wife, secured permission for his ashes to be placed behind the altar in St George's Chapel, Windsor, where those of his mother and father also lay.

'I say. You're a very good swimmer. Who are you?' 'Johnny Weismuller' was the reply

Edwardes–Berman Doubles Trophy

In 1973 a small South African named Toddy Berman, who was then in his mid-forties and had been an outstanding squash player, arrived in Britain and joined the Club. He knew a number of members because he had met Brian Phillips when an SRA team toured South Africa in 1955, and Jack Giles when Giles visited in 1956. So there was only one club for Toddy to join when he came to live in London and wanted to play squash and that was the Royal Automobile Club.

Not long after arriving in London, Toddy was introduced by Jack Giles to Michael Edwardes, a fellow countryman, who was also a member. A strong friendship began

Michael Edwardes (left) and Toddy Berman, donors of the Edwardes–Berman Doubles Trophy, were a formidable doubles team. Here they show off the GB Vets Club Over 65s doubles trophy, having a few years earlier also won the Over 55s competition.

between the two South Africans that continues to this day. At singles squash Edwardes was no match for Berman, so the two of them paired up and began playing doubles on a singles court at Pall Mall. One day one of them said to the other, 'We ought to have a doubles competition here. The members would like it. Why don't we start one?'

But before the annual doubles competition could start, a trophy was needed. Edwardes delegated the task to Berman. 'I walked down Regent Street and into Garrards, who I believe were the Queen's jewellers, and started talking to them about a trophy,' said Berman. 'It was specially made for us and took two or three months, if my memory serves. I made several visits to Garrards to chivvy them along.'

The Edwardes–Berman Doubles Trophy is an unusual design, consisting of a solid wood rectangular plaque bearing a sculpture in silver of four players on its

We ought to have a doubles competition here. The members would like it. Why don't we start one?

Darren Johnson with the Edwardes–Berman Doubles Trophy in 2005. Johnson won not only the doubles that year, in partnership with Grant Miller, but also the Open. Only Chris Orriss in 1982 had previously achieved this 'double'.

front and set on a wooden base. It is perhaps eight inches wide and six inches tall. Toddy Berman was so anxious to make sure that the squash players looked realistic that he got Jack Giles to approve it before the work was completed. The annual doubles competition is open to all-comers and all ages. 'Michael and I never won it but Clifford Leuw and my son Raoul did in the second year after we presented it.'

Canada Cup

The Canada Cup is a striking trophy, distinctive for its having three handles. It is awarded not to the winner of a competition, as the others are, but to the member who, in the opinion of the professionals, has best demonstrated the spirit of Pall Mall and of squash in the previous year. It is the gift of Peter Wright, who was born in Toronto, came to Britain to work in London for nearly 13 years in the 1980s and 1990s and became a British citizen before returning to Canada.

'I arrived in London in the autumn of 1987 and had my first day of work in the City at the Canadian Imperial Bank of Commerce, near Tower Bridge, on the day of the October market crash,' Wright said. 'I also worked in the City for the likes of Merrill Lynch, Bankers Trust and Robert Fleming while I was there. The Club became my "home" in 1992 or

I presented the cup to the Club as a thank you for the wonderful memories I had of squash there

The Canada Cup is presented annually to the member who best embodies the spirit of Pall Mall during the year. The winner in 2004 was Victor Chung.

1993 and I was active in the leagues there, playing at the same level as Guy Darby. It was where I played what I call my main squash.

'When I returned to Canada I presented the cup to the Club as a thank you for the wonderful memories I had of squash there. I treasure memories of the friendliness to me of Greg and Mark and of the sports staff including Sunny, who is no longer there, and Herbie, who still is! It was also a mark of the appreciation I felt for being able to bring my Canadian guests to the Club to share in the history and the old world charm it offered. In particular I loved taking people to the Great Gallery. I spent a few nights playing snooker in the basement. I also used the golf facility in Epsom and have a special memory of sharing a round with my 80-year-old mother for her birthday that year!

'I bought the cup in Portobello Road market in west London. I think it cost me roughly 50 quid. I had it engraved separately and chose to call it the Canada Cup to keep it simple and remind everyone of the special bonds between our countries. My father served in the Royal Navy and I became a British citizen after five years in the UK and I see this as a very proud personal accomplishment in my life. I left to return to Canada at Easter in 2000 just before the dinner at which the Canada Cup was presented for the first time.'

I bought the cup in Portobello Road market in west London. I think it cost me roughly 50 quid

Afterword

The six preceding chapters celebrate squash at Pall Mall as a competitive and recreational game. They should have given a flavour of the sport's history inside and outside the Royal Automobile Club as well as telling you a lot about squash's place at the Club and the people who teach it and play it there. In reading these chapters you will likely have been reacquainted with members whose names are familiar – but also introduced to many you didn't know.

In his message at the front of this book, James Sandwith, the current chairman of the squash committee, wrote of the things that make squash at our club special. He wrote, 'It's the context in which it's played: the people, the surroundings, the drinks, the laughs, the stories, the continuity, the spirit.'

It is for just those reasons that the basement area at Pall Mall is so beloved, and has been since 1911. Go down there now and what do you hear? The crack of squash balls, the hubbub of conversation, the sound of laughter. They have been present for 100 years. May they be so for another 100.

The Squash Committee

The squash committee at the time of writing. Back row (left to right): Maurice Glover, Simon Lambert, Michael Metcalfe, Dominic Curtis. Seated: Greg Lamond, James Sandwith, Chris Orriss. Right (absent from main photograph): Nick Clapp, Graham Nichols.

AGE-GROUP COMPETITIONS

Season	Veterans – Over 45 The Lowenthal Trophy	Veterans – Over 55 The Herbert Cup	Veterans – Over 65 The Stainton Cup
1975/76	T. Berman		
1976/77	D. Thompson		
1977/78	W.D.N. Vaughan	B.C. Phillips	
1978/79	T. Berman	J.W. Roche	
1979/80	W.D.N. Vaughan	A.W.R. Baddeley	
1980/81	T. Berman	L. Lowenthal	
1981/82	C.D. Leuw	W.D.N. Vaughan	
1982/83	M.W. Breckon	W.D.N. Vaughan	
1983/84	P.H. Chalk	W.D.N. Vaughan	
1984/85	P.H. Chalk	T. Berman	
1985/86	P. Armstrong	T. Berman	
1986/87	T. Wedgworth	D. Allen	
1987/88	M.J. Perkins	M.J. Perkins	
1988/89	P.H. Chalk	M.J. Perkins	
1989/90	P.O. Brown	M.J. Perkins	
1990/91	P.H. Chalk	P.H. Chalk	
1991/92	N.J. Faulks	M.J. Perkins	
1992/93	N.J. Faulks	P.O. Brown	
1993/94	N.J. Faulks	P.H. Chalk	
1994/95	N.J. Faulks	P.F.D. Trimingham	T. Berman
1995/96	R.G. Ford	M.J. Perkins	D. Allen
1996/97	R.G. Ford	D.R. Esser	M.J. Perkins
1997/98	S.H. Courtney	D.R. Esser	M.J. Perkins
1998/99	S.H. Courtney	D.R. Esser	M.J. Perkins
1999/00	K. Bush	J.R. Beatles	P.H. Chalk
2000/01	K. Bush	R.D. Trimingham	A.A. Peirce
2001/02	S.H. Courtney	D.R. Esser	A.A. Peirce
2002/03	S.H. Courtney	P.A. Ventham	A.A. Peirce
2003/04	S.H. Courtney	D.R. Esser	P.F.D. Trimingham
2004/05	P. Bourdon	S.H. Courtney	P.O. Brown
2005/06	P. Bourdon	R.G. Ford	D. Mawson
2006/07	G.T. Mitchell	R.G. Ford	D. Mawson
2007/08	A.G. Nicholson	G.T. Mitchell	D. Mawson
2008/09	A.G. Nicholson	K. Bush	D. Mawson
2009/10	A.G. Nicholson	A.S. Lowenthal	D. Mawson

DOUBLES COMPETITIONS

Season	Open Doubles – The Edwardes–Berman Trophy	Season	Open Doubles – The Edwardes–Berman Trophy
1981/82	C. Orriss F.R. Watts	1986/87	T.J.C. Jenkins D. Weston
1982/83	R. Berman C.D. Leuw	1987/88	C. Orriss F.R. Watts
1983/84	C. Orriss F.R. Watts	1988/89	S.M. Lambert C.F. Stokes
1984/85	W.R. Triggs P.F.D. Trimingham	1989/90	S.M. Lambert C.F. Stokes
1985/86	C. Orriss F.R. Watts	1990/91	C. Orriss F.R. Watts

Season	Open Doubles – The Edwardes–Berman Trophy		Season	Open Doubles – The Edwardes–Berman Trophy	Handicap Doubles
1991/92	W.R. Triggs P.F.D. Trimingham		2001/02	A. Ezra J. Sandwith	
1992/93	M.J. Birkin C. Orriss		2002/03	G. Miller D.B. Johnson	
1993/94	M.J. Birkin C. Orriss		2003/04	S.H. Courtney M.G. Lees	V.C. Chung P.A. Ventham
1994/95	J. Bewes J.R. Rogerson		2004/05	G. Miller D.B. Johnson	M.R. Jackson G.T. Mitchell
1995/96	M.J. Birkin C. Orriss		2005/06	A. Ezra J. Sandwith	G.A. Gelardi C.J. Lowry
1996/97	G.W. Nielsen A.D. Stimpson		2006/07	A. Ezra J. Sandwith	D.G. Wright A.J. Meyer
1997/98	G.W. Nielsen A.D. Stimpson		2007/08	A. Ezra J. Sandwith	V.C. Chung P.A. Ventham
1998/99	G.W. Nielsen A.D. Stimpson		2008/09	A. Ezra J. Sandwith	G.G. Macpherson N. McMahon
1999/00	S.H. Courtney M.G. Lees		2009/10	A. Ezra J. Sandwith	V.C. Chung P.A. Ventham
2000/01	G.P. Brocklesby C.J. Lowry				

THE CANADA CUP

Season	Winner		Season	Winner
1999/00	M. Winter		2005/06	H. Caseley
2000/01	D. Rawle		2006/07	P. Hillman
2001/02	D. Humphrys		2007/08	S. McGivern
2002/03	A. Franks		2008/09	G. Gelardi
2003/04	V. Chung		2009/10	J. Maskey
2004/05	G. Nichols			

INTERNATIONALS

Name	Representing	Debut	Last Match	Appearances
Amr Bey, F.D.	England	1935	1935	1
Basset, W.F.	England	1923	1927	5
Brazier, D.R.	England	1966	1967	4*
	Great Britain	1967	1967	
Broomfield, N.H.R.A.	England	1955	1961	13*
	Great Britain	1956	1959	
Campbell, C.N.	Scotland	1951	1953	9
Corby, M.W.	England	1962	1975	41*
	Great Britain	1967	1971	
Courtney, S.H.	England	1971	1980	26*
	Great Britain	1972	1976	
Dagnall, H.J.A.	England	1948	1949	3
Doyle, J.W.	Ireland	1954	1962	9
Dugdale, D.R.	England	1948	1948	1
Drysdale, I.	England	1923	1923	2
Easter, J.N.C.	England	1971	1982	31*
	Great Britain	1970	1973	

* Combined number of appearances for home nation and Great Britain.

* Combined number of appearances for home nation and Great Britain.

Name	Representing	Debut	Last Match	Appearances
Ezra, A.	India	1987	1995	n/k
Gathercole, T.D.	England	1962	1966	14*
	Great Britain	1962	1965	
Hildick-Smith, G.	South Africa	1950	n/k	n/k
Hodgson, D.L.	South Africa	1953	n/k	n/k
Ispahani, S.A.	England	1970	1970	2
	India	1971	n/k	n/k
Leslie, J.C.A.	England	1974	1979	42*
	Great Britain	1976	1979	
Lloyd, C.J.C.	Wales	1969	1972	12
Lowe, P.F.	Wales	1969	1969	3
Massy, G.D.	England	1963	1965	12*
	Great Britain	1963	1965	
Oddy, M.A.	Scotland	1954	1972	35*
	Great Britain	1956	1962	
Perkins, M.J.	England	1955	1958	9*
	Great Britain	1955	1955	
Phillips, B.C.	England	1947	1955	13*
	Great Britain	1955	1955	
Phillips, P.J.	England	1949	1949	1
Ridgers, J.N.S.	England	1935	1935	1
Strawson, F.M.	England	1926	1937	3
Verney, L.J.	Wales	1949	1965	44

THE DRYSDALE CUP

Season	Winner	From	Season	Winner	From
1925/26	C.J. Wilson	Repton	1955/56	M.A. Oddy	Late Rugby
1926/27	C.J. Wilson	Repton	1956/57	D. Jude	Late Lancing
1927/28	K.A. Wagg	Eton	1957/58	D.I. Medway	Late Cheltenham
1928/29	J.N.S. Ridgers	Wellington	1958/59	M.W. Corby	Mill Hill
1929/30	E.N. Evans	Haileybury	1959/60	D.R. Brazier	Lancing
1930/31	J.A. Gillies	Winchester	1960/61	P. Gerlow	Denmark
1931/32	R.W. Beadle	Marlborough	1961/62	P. Gerlow	Denmark
1932/33	N.W.D. Yardley	St. Peter's	1962/63	M.S. Khan	Millfield
1933/34	N.W.D. Yardley	St. Peter's	1963/64	B. Patterson	Barnard Castle
1934/35	G.S. Panchaud	Lancing	1964/65	A. Nayar	India
1935/36	C.M. Butler	Lancing	1965/66	C. Orriss	Late Hymers
1936/37	R.S. Woodward	Lancing	1966/67	S.H. Courtney	City of London
1937/38	D.G. Yeats Brown	Tonbridge	1967/68	S.H. Courtney	City of London
1938/39	A.G. Aitchison	Cranleigh	1968/69	J.L. Richardson	Hurstpierpoint
1939/40 to 1945/46	No Competition		1969/70	P.G. Verow	Barnard Castle
			1970/71	M. Khan	Pakistan
1946/47	J.R. Barrington	Brighton	1971/72	P.G. Verow	Late Barnard Castle
1947/48	D.A. Swales	Lancing	1972/73	B.K. O'Connor	Peckham Manor
1948/49	M.G. Case	Marlborough	1973/74	P.S. Kenyon	Late Blackpool College
1949/50	M.G. Case	Marlborough	1974/75	P.S. Kenyon	Late Blackpool College
1950/51	W.J. Downey	Sedbergh	1975/76	G. Briars	Gresham's
1951/52	N.H.R.A. Broomfield	Haileybury	1976/77	G. Briars	Gresham's
1952/53	J.G.A. Lyon	Lancing	1977/78	G. Brumby	Australia
1953/54	N.H.R.A. Broomfield	Haileybury	1978/79	G. Brumby	Australia
1954/55	N.H.R.A. Broomfield	Haileybury	1979/80	S. Davenport	New Zealand

Season	Winner	From		Season	Winner	From
1980/81	S. Qaiser	Pakistan		1996/97	A. Faizy	Egypt
1981/82	C. Dittmar	Australia		1997/98	B. Ong Ben Hee	Malaysia
1982/83	J. Hickox	Surrey		1998/99	N. Matthew	Yorkshire
1983/84	D. Lloyd	Shropshire		1999/00	K. Darwish	Egypt
1984/85	D. Harris	Essex		2000/01	G. Gaultier	France
1985/86	D. Harris	Essex		2001/02	J. Willstrop	Yorkshire
1986/87	D. Harris	Essex		2002/03	S. Khan	Pakistan
1987/88	D. Harris	Essex		2003/04	S. Ghosal	India
1988/89	S. Parke	Yorkshire		2004/05	B. Ashfaq	Pakistan
1989/90	P. Marshall	Leicestershire		2005/06	R. Ashour	Egypt
1990/91	S. Parke	Yorkshire		2006/07	O. Mosaad	Egypt
1991/92	J. Raumolin	Finland		2007/08	M. El Shorbagy	Egypt
1992/93	J. Rennie	Cheshire		2008/09	M. El Shorbagy	Egypt
1993/94	A. Barada	Egypt		2009/10	M. El Shorbagy	Egypt
1994/95	I. Higgins	Essex		2010/11	A. Farag	Egypt
1995/96	A. Faizy	Egypt				

THE BATH CLUB CUP COMPETITION ROLL OF HONOUR

Season	Division 1	Division 2	Division 3 (Veterans Division from 1999/00)
1922/23	Royal Automobile Club		
1923/24	Bath Club		
1924/25	Bath Club		
1925/26	Queen's Club		
1926/27	Royal Automobile Club		
1927/28	R.A.F.		
1928/29	Bath Club		
1929/30	Queen's Club	Prince's	
1930/31	Queen's Club	Conservative	Naval & Military
1931/32	Queen's Club	M.C.C.	*No Competition*
1932/33	Royal Automobile Club	Bachelor's	Royal Aero Club
1933/34	Bath Club	Prince's	United Service
1934/35	Royal Automobile Club	Bachelor's	Union
1935/36	Queen's Club	Royal Aero Club	Naval & Military
1936/37	Conservative	Bachelor's	United Service
1937/38	Conservative	Union	Caledonian
1938/39	Queen's Club	R.A.F.	*No Competition*
1939/40 to 1945/46	*No Competition*		
1946/47	Royal Automobile Club	*No Competition*	*No Competition*
1947/48	Queen's Club	*No Competition*	*No Competition*
1948/49	Royal Automobile Club	M.C.C.	Union
1949/50	M.C.C.	Bath Club	R.A.F.
1950/51	Royal Automobile Club	Conservative	Guards
1951/52	Royal Automobile Club	Queen's Club	Hurlingham
1952/53	Junior Carlton	Bath Club	United Service
1953/54	Royal Automobile Club	Hurlingham	Guards
1954/55	M.C.C.	Bath Club	Queen's Club
1955/56	M.C.C.	Queen's Club	R.A.F.
1956/57	Junior Carlton	Lansdowne Club	East India & Sports
1957/58	Junior Carlton	Royal Automobile Club	R.A.F.

Season	Division 1	Division 2	Division 3 (Veterans Division from 1999/00)
1958/59	Junior Carlton	Bath Club	United Service
1959/60	M.C.C.	Lansdowne Club	East India & Sports
1960/61	Junior Carlton	Royal Automobile Club	United Service
1961/62	Royal Automobile Club	Bath Club	Guards
1962/63	Royal Automobile Club	Hurlingham	Public Schools
1963/64	Royal Automobile Club	Bath Club	United University
1964/65	Royal Automobile Club	Public Schools	Naval & Military
1965/66	Royal Automobile Club	Bath Club	R.A.F.
1966/67	Lansdowne Club	Hurlingham	Cavalry
1967/68	Lansdowne Club	Bath Club	Junior Carlton
1968/69	Lansdowne Club	Hurlingham	East India & Sports
1969/70	Lansdowne Club	Junior Carlton	*No Competition*
1970/71	Bath Club	M.C.C.	
1971/72	Queen's Club	Royal Automobile Club	
1972/73	Queen's Club	United University	
1973/74	East India & Sports	Hurlingham	
1974/75	Queen's Club	Bath Club	
1975/76	Hurlingham	Queen's Club II	
1976/77	Queen's Club	Bath Club	
1977/78	Queen's Club	Queen's Club II	
1978/79	Queen's Club	Junior Carlton	
1979/80	Queen's Club	Queen's Club II	
1980/81	Queen's Club	United Oxford & Cambridge	
1981/82	East India & Sports	Queen's Club II	
1982/83	East India & Sports	Naval & Military	
1983/84	Royal Automobile Club	Royal Automobile Club II	
1984/85	Queen's Club	H.A.C.	
1985/86	East India & Sports	Cavalry	
1986/87	Queen's Club	Royal Automobile Club II	
1987/88	East India & Sports	Royal Automobile Club II	
1988/89	Lamb's	Queen's Club II	
1989/90	United Oxford & Cambridge	Queen's Club II	
1990/91	Queen's Club	H.A.C.	
1991/92	Cotton's	Bath & Racquets Club	
1992/93	Queen's Club	Royal Automobile Club II	
1993/94	Bath & Racquets Club	Royal Automobile Club II	
1994/95	Bath & Racquets Club	Royal Automobile Club II	
1995/96	Bath & Racquets Club	Lansdowne Club	
1996/97	Bath & Racquets Club	Queen's Club II	
1997/98	Bath & Racquets Club	United Oxford & Cambridge III	
1998/99	Bath & Racquets Club	Hurlingham II	
1999/00	Bath & Racquets Club	Cumberland Club	Royal Automobile Club
2000/01	Cumberland Club	Cumberland Club II	Cumberland Club
2001/02	Bath & Racquets Club	Naval & Military	Royal Automobile Club
2002/03	Bath & Racquets Club	Queen's Club III	Royal Automobile Club
2003/04	M.C.C.	Cumberland Club II	Royal Automobile Club
2004/05	Bath & Racquets Club	Hurlingham III	Queen's Club
2005/06	Queen's Club	Royal Automobile Club II	Roehampton
2006/07	Lamb's	Royal Automobile Club II	M.C.C
2007/08	H.A.C.	Queen's Club II	M.C.C
2008/09	H.A.C.	Cumberland Club II	M.C.C
2009/10	Lansdowne Club	Lansdowne Club II	M.C.C